Perishable

Perishable

A Memoir

Dirk Jamison

Library of Congress Cataloging-in-Publication Data
Jamison, Dirk.
Perishable : a memoir / Dirk Jamison.—1st ed.
p. cm.
ISBN 1-55652-599-0
1. Jamison, Dirk—Childhood and youth. 2. Children of un-
    employed parents—California—Biography. 3. Children of
    unemployed parents—Oregon—Biography. 4. Mormons—
    California—Biography. 5. Mormons—Oregon—Biography.
    6. California—Biography. 7. Oregon—Biography. I. Title.
CT275.J2965A3 2006
979.4'94—dc22   2005028357

Cover and interior design: Emily Brackett, Visible Logic
All photos are from the author's private collection.

Portions of this book have previously appeared in
substantially different form in the *LA Weekly*, the *Utne Reader*,
the *New Internationalist Magazine*, and on Public Radio
International's *This American Life*.

First edition
Published by Chicago Review Press, Incorporated
814 North Franklin Street
Chicago, Illinois 60610
ISBN-10: 1-55652-599-0
ISBN-13: 978-1-55652-599-5
Printed in the United States of America
5 4 3 2 1

Contents

Perishable

Part One
Huntington Beach, California, 1973

Chapter 1

Mother makes a birthday cake from scratch, then decorates it with little marzipan Eskimos standing in marzipan canoes. She's using her shoulder to pin the telephone against her ear. The cake is huge, and so is she. The cake is for me.

She tells the phone this:

"Now with me, you start cutting from the end of the watermelon and everyone has a slice. His way is to cut down the middle and eat the heart out, because that's the part he wants. I told him he's being selfish. The heart is the best part, and you should only take your share of the best part. But he says he can take whatever he wants."

She's talking about Dad. Her tone of voice suggests that the phone line leads to one of her Mormon sisters living in Oregon. It's the third time she's told this story today.

"I warned him not to do it again, but you know him. He did it again. So I picked up the melon and went after him. He could see that I was gonna throw it, so he started running. He ran right out of the house, and I hit him in the head while he was on the steps. But it didn't make a difference. He did it again today. I keep thinking he's going to evolve, that these weirdnesses in him are going to change. But it keeps getting worse instead of better."

For each sister, at some point, Mother whispers "midlife crisis" so I decide to say something as she hangs up. I use the phrase Dad got from Carlos Castaneda.

"What?" She repositions one of the Eskimo's arms, then starts streaking the river blue with food dye on a toothpick.

"You said 'midlife crisis' again. He says it's a Path with Heart."

"What?"

"Dad calls it a Path with Heart."

There's purple frosting at the corner of her mouth, and she's staring at me, almost cross-eyed. I get the feeling I usually get when she stares. I wonder whether she's forgotten my name.

"Oh, honey," Mother says, with . . . I'm not sure what it is. Pity? Disappointment? She uses the toothpick to jab the Eskimo two blue eyes, then goes to her room to cry for a while.

✦

Dad tucks us in. My older sister always gets an "abalone story" from his days as a professional scuba diver. For my little brother, it's a memorized list of tropical vacations:

"Where we going at three, Daddy?"

"Hawaii."

"Four?"

"Belize."

"Five?"

"Cancún."

These are the places he will take us. One paradise per hour.

I get a kiss on the forehead, and the same thing whispered every night. "I wanna be like you when I grow up."

But then that insomniac poke after what always feels like only a couple minutes. It's two in the morning and Dad hasn't slept for weeks. "Happy birthday," he whispers. "You feel like walking?"

We head to the beach so he can tell me a few things. Free will versus Determinism. Nature versus Nurture. Society versus the Individual. There's always a versus, and his favorite is Male versus Female. I understand maybe a tenth of it because I'm seven, but one thing is clear. He's not happy.

We go to our usual perch on the deck of lifeguard station #7. The boardwalk is lined with towering palm trees, all leaning too far in the same direction. Someday they'll all tip over. It's freezing, and there's a tractor-sized grooming machine cruising parallel with the water. Dad gives me his jacket, then reads me his latest poem. His money diary has turned into a book of poetry—*The Messiah's Handbook: Feet of Clay Walking in Shoes of Arrogance*. It's a ledger book with graph paper. He used to keep track of money made and spent while diving for abalone, so old entries generally go something like this:

> Minney's swap meet. Pulley and rope—$2.

New entries sound more like this:

> God abhors the goodness of man
> it stinks to heaven
> making the pure places rotten
> paths obscure
> plucking the seeing eyes and rolling
> them in offal
> 'til a whited image is left a monument
> to Satan.

I ask him, "What's offal?"
"Feces."
"What's feces?"
"Human shit."
"Ah."

✳

Dad says, "Poor bastard," as the grooming machine passes. A spotlight above the deck shows us the driver slumped forward like he's dead. Dad is counting weeks like he used to count days. His life has become a tedious holding pattern where nothing adds up. He doesn't bother washing his pants anymore. They just get dirty again the next day. His wife is a massive jack-Mormon wrapped in polyester who can't take a single sentence at face value. "If I say two words, she hears six!"

A jack-Mormon is a member who no longer spends time in an actual church. Mother considers herself a serious believer prevented from worshipping by a godless husband who thinks Mormons have no brains.

Dad gave her a Soap-on-a-Rope in the shape of an aspirin because that's what she swallows at night to sleep. Just a joke. But Mother warned me that the oversized pill meant her husband wanted her to "go to sleep for good." Once, in a crowded mall, Dad let go of a door and nailed her in the head. Just an accident. But rather than accuse him of being impolite, Mother stunned shoppers with the accusation that her husband was trying to kill her with public doors.

She's a little sensitive lately. She's still trying to recover from her discovery of a list a few months ago. An *Enemies* list. Written by Dad during a night panic, then hidden in plain sight on the bedside dresser. The list was long, and Mother is working on forgetting about it. But she's having trouble forgetting the first two items listed:

    1. Wife

    2. Kids

✸

Dad describes *The Virtue of Selfishness,* by Ayn Rand, which claims that the word *selfish* was invented in order to push people around.

"When you hear that word, you gotta pay attention. It means somebody wants to keep you from doing what you want. *Self-interest* is a better word since it's impossible *not* to act in your own self-interest. Even when you work like a dog for other people, it's still for you. So why not just do the things you like?"

It seems like a chance to mention it, so I do. "Like eating the watermelon heart."

"Exactly!" He's quiet a moment. "What did she tell you about that?"

"Nothing."

"She threw the damn thing at me. Did she tell you that? And I got another watermelon just for her. Did she tell you that? I even said to her, 'Now I want *you* to eat the heart.' I wanted her to experience that same thing I did. You've got this really great part! I wanted her to experience the heart of life, I guess. You give yourself that gift. The gift of what happens. And that's what makes life worthwhile. But she wouldn't do it. I said, 'This one's just for you. You eat the heart!' She said, 'I can't. I can't eat the heart.' She couldn't eat the heart! Even if I cut it out and gave it to her, she still couldn't eat it. And I don't know why. I guess she doesn't think she deserves it. That's probably why."

*

Dad tucks me in again and wishes me luck on our dreaming project. His goal is to expand our "cognizant minds" by controlling our dreams, which will allegedly encourage the merging of the unconscious and conscious. "Good luck," he says.

Mother suggested that dreams serve a purpose. "So you shouldn't mess with them."

"Jesus," Dad said. "Of course we should mess with them!"

The first step is to simply acknowledge the dream state. *I am dreaming.* Then you look around to identify your location.

This is usually what trips Dad up. It's the third step that gets me. You look at your hands, which initiates a new transitional state just beneath consciousness. You're supposed to float there, but I always jolt awake, already in a sitting position and looking at what I assume are my real hands. It's a feeling similar to tipping over backward in a chair.

There are seven total steps. Once we get through them all, Dad says, we can spend all night doing whatever the hell we want.

*

Tonight's dream is this:

I'm treading water in the ocean when a cartoon whale surfaces and starts chasing me. His teeth are tree stumps made of cement. I say to myself, do not piss your pants. You are only dreaming. Just swim faster than possible. But there's no shore, so I decide to fly instead. I don't flap my arms. I just glide. Then I remember to look at my damn hands, and plunge horribly into my real bed.

Dad is getting ready for work in the kitchen. The sun is starting to show. I tell him about the dream.

"Christ, really?" he says. "That's fantastic!"

"Shhh."

"The flying is step four," he says. "You made a conscious decision in your unconscious. The only problem is that it came before step three. So next time, look at your hands just for a second, then look away. Don't stare at them. That's when you get stuck."

He empties his carpenter's pouch onto the counter. Nails, screws, drill bits, sawdust. "Hey, you know what birthdays are for? So you can take stock. You stop and ask yourself, How's this life thing going so far?" He clips the carpenter's belt around his waist, then uses scissors to open a jumbo bag of sunflower seeds. "So how's it going?"

"Huh?"

"How's it going?"

"Me?"

"Yeah."

"Pretty good."

"Yeah? Because I've been thinking about something my grandfather said. He had a heart attack waiting for a bus. I told you that, right? He just laid back on the grass and died. But he told me something a couple days earlier. He said, 'We shit on life, then wonder why it stinks.'"

The carpenter's belt has three separate pouches. Dad fills all three with sunflower seeds. "That seems very pertinent to me lately."

"What's *pertinent* mean?"

"It's like when you say something speaks volumes. Or it just means that's how I feel. But don't worry. I have a plan." He pats one of the pouches bulging with seeds. "In fact, why don't you come to work with me?"

"I have school."

"That doesn't matter. It'll be fun. That's one hell of a birthday cake, huh?"

It's on the kitchen table. There's an entire second tier now. It looks like a wedding cake. There are dozens of cheerful arctic characters. Orcas, otters, dolphins. But Mother has added clubs to the hands of the Eskimos. The clubs are raised over their heads, and they've cornered a marzipan walrus.

Chapter 2

The job site is a half-finished restaurant called The Spaghetti Factory in Newport Beach. Dad stuffs his cheek with the sunflower seeds and waits for the foreman to catch us sitting in a corner. He describes a scene from a Carlos Castaneda book that Mother calls "the butterfly book." She blames this book for teaching her husband how to "ignore all the rules." When she first noticed a change in him, he was carrying a paperback copy around constantly, and there was a butterfly on the cover.

Dad's description of the scene gets interrupted by a carpenter wearing a baseball cap backward. He stops to stare at us. "You brought your kid on the job?"

"That's right," Dad says. "He can control his dreams."

"What?"

"He controls his dreams."

"Is that good?"

"Jesus, Lou, nice talking to you."

"What, I just don't understand what you're telling me."

"Yeah, I noticed. Go back to work."

"Look who's talking!"

In the scene, a mentor is trying to show his apprentice how to broaden his reality by sitting in a desert and just looking around for days at a time. When the apprentice sees a giant lion-faced lizard breathing fire behind a bush, he points with great excitement, then realizes that it's nothing. Just a plastic bag caught on the bush, thrashing in the breeze. He laughs and describes what he thought he saw.

The mentor tells him, "Well, you had it right for a second there."

✳

Dad's best friend shows up late with a hangover. His black hair is even shaggier than usual, and his handlebar mustache, which is usually twisted into points, looks like two sparrow wings. His name is Bob K——— but that has to change soon because he's in trouble for crashing motorcycles, then walking home. If he stayed, he would get arrested for drunk driving, which is far more expensive than the motorcycles he abandons. He only drives pieces of crap registered under fake names. Something didn't work right this time, though, because now the police are after him.

While Bob hammers, Dad disputes the existence of a grocery store across the street.

Bob says, "What the hell are you talking about? It's right there."

"How can you be so sure?"

"I see it. Right there."

"Yeah, I see something."

"Look at the sign! It's says Stater Bros."

"Yeah, I see that too. But I'm not convinced."

"Christ . . ."

Dad climbs a ladder to graffiti a steel beam with an orange carpenter's crayon. He writes what his grandfather said about shitting on life, then cups his hands like a bullhorn and addresses the crew. "I wrote down a little wisdom for you miserable sons a bitches!"

A few carpenters laugh.

Dad sits atop the ladder and begins spitting sunflower shells on the floor while singing this song:

"If you wanna be happy for the rest of your life, never make a pretty woman your wife. So from my personal point of view, get an ugly girl to marry you."

Someone shouts, "Take a day off, man. You're losing it!"

"Hey, shut up down there! I'm in charge now. So somebody better sweep up these godawful sunflower seeds!"

Bob slaps his knees when he laughs, sometimes rocking back and forth, depending on how funny something is. It's one of the reasons I like Bob. He laughs so hard, it looks like he's going crazy.

When the foreman finally peeks in, Dad is lifting his first hammer of the day, to smash a hornet on a floor joist overhead. The foreman heads back to his boss trailer without Dad even noticing him, which gets Bob laughing again.

"What?" Dad laughs a little without knowing why. Bob's laugh has this effect on people.

Bob tells him about the foreman.

Dad comes down off the ladder. "Christ Almighty." This is one of his favorite things to say. "Jesus Christ on a goddamn crutch" is another.

*

We go to Bob's bungalow apartment for lunch and advice on getting fired. Dad has lost so many jobs without trying, he figures doing it on purpose will be a cinch.

Every time he works with Bob, they get canned. On their last job, plywood sheets were being peeled from a concrete wall with a huge crane. It was six stories up, and the bosses expected the carpenters to stand directly next to the action and

help. Ernie was a friend who had gotten them the work. He
was the only one dumb enough to do it:

"So Ernie's up there working like a madman. Bob and I
are on the ground laughing. Then he gets knocked off balance
and goes swinging out with the plywood. Just hanging on
with his hands! It was crazy. We wouldn't even go up there, let
alone work on the edge of the building like that. They expect
you to risk your life for some silly job."

But that's not why they got fired.

"No, it's because we were laughing too much. That happens a lot."

✦

From his front porch, Bob gives driving advice instead: never
stop your car for a woman waiting to cross the street.

If you just zoom past, the woman will hurry home to offer
her husband or boyfriend intercourse. She will do this to mask
the injury of you not liking her enough to stop your car and
study the way she walks. Each time Bob does this, he imag-
ines what the intercourse she's about to give will look like. He
claims it's better than finding out how she walks. And it feels
good to help his fellow man get some tail. He feels a sense of
brotherhood because tail is so difficult to get.

✦

A neighbor woman starts moving stones around. Bob's driveway is outlined with stones that people have kicked out of position. The woman is putting them back into a nice curve, but she keeps glaring over at us. Bob whispers that it's because the driveway is shared by all the tenants. The rocks also belong to Bob, and the woman is upset because the men aren't helping.

Dad calls to the woman, "It's OK not to do something."

She squints. "What?"

"It's OK *not* to do something."

"What?"

"You heard me."

"Hey," Bob says, "don't aggravate these people. I have to live here." Then he offers to narc. He used Dad as an impartial reference to get the job, so the foreman is unaware of their friendship. Bob can turn him in for swiping lumber after dark.

"I wanna get fired, not arrested." Dad goes down to the driveway, but not to help the woman.

Bob says, "How about I just tell the him the truth? You're a lazy shit."

"That sounds about right." Dad starts picking up cigarette

butts. Bob smokes like a fiend, and tosses each butt directly in front of his home.

Bob says, "What the hell are you doing that for?"

Dad thinks a moment. "It's OK *not* to do something. And it's OK to *do* something." He addresses the woman again. "Right?"

"What?"

"It's OK to *do* something."

She hurries inside.

Bob slaps his knee. "She hates your guts."

"No. She's just shy."

＊

Dad dresses up like a pirate for my birthday dinner because he doesn't have an Eskimo costume. He says "arg" as I blow out the candles. Then he tilts up his eye patch and opens a mason jar full of banana wine that's been brewing above the fridge for two weeks. He wants to celebrate an "important decision" that none of us bother asking about. He won't tell anyway. He prefers to spring things on you when you aren't asking. Bob gave him the wine recipe. It smells like vinegar. Dad drinks half the jar, then goes outside to vomit repeatedly.

Mother picks up the telephone. I figure she's calling a doctor because Dad has poisoned himself, but she says, "My way is to start cutting from the end of the melon, and everyone has a slice. . . ."

I go to the front porch to watch Dad roll around on the lawn.

"Dad?"

"Oh my God."

He digs his fingers into grass and claims that the lawn is vertical. He thinks he's dangling from the edge of the world.

✻

The sound of a helicopter carries me from my bed to the window. Dad is now rolling on the backyard patio in the moonlight, groaning and pounding the concrete with his fists. This must be a dream. Dad is nude. It's a police helicopter circling the house. When they hit Dad with a floodlight, he rises up and offers both his middle fingers. Wiener and balls wagging. The police don't seem to understand his gesture. They don't leave, so Dad picks up a rock the size of a ping-pong ball and prepares to throw.

It's not a dream. I run to the back door, thinking his skull is about to be scattered like those shards of melon on the steps. But police apparently understand rocks. The helicopter tilts and floats away.

Dad comes inside. "You feel like walking?"

"What's going on?"

"Goddamn pigs," he explains.

*

He decides, at the last second, to wear clothes to the beach. There's the usual fog, but something smells this time. A black lump ahead of us on the sand. It looks like something washed up. Dad pulls out a brochure. "Get a load of this." He loves to ski, and Mammoth Mountain apparently has the most square footage of terrifying slope in America. The brochure features a gondola racing to a peak called the Cornice, where skiers are shown peering over a cliff, realizing they must take a significant free fall before the actual skiing can begin. Halfway down the mountain is a café where they can collapse and reward themselves with monstrous steins of beer.

Dad says, "Looks good, huh? I say we move to a ski resort and have a blast. Why not? We can ski or whatever. I'll get unemployment. That'll carry us through winter, and there's always food stamps. All I need to do is lose my job and we'll be cooking with gasoline, right? Why not?"

The answer is so obvious, I figure he's just talking to himself. Or maybe he expects me to do something. At least say something. He never has these kind of conversations with my brother or sister. What does he expect me to do?

Pay close attention, I tell myself.

Good idea.

The lump is a dead seal at the edge of the water. Bloated and wearing sunglasses made of flies.

"Seriously," Dad says. "Why not?"

"Mom."

"Exactly! But I don't care any more. You know? This isn't working the way it is." He prods the seal belly with his boot, sending the flies into a momentary frenzy. The stink is breathtaking.

Chapter 3

Mother likes to invite ten-speed missionaries into the house for lunch, so Dad taught us to scatter like deer when the doorbell rings.

Dad wants a no-chore policy, to give his children a feeling of "agency," so Mother turned bed making and dishwashing into contests with pie as reward.

Mother wanted me to attend kindergarten, so Dad encouraged me to play permanent hooky. "I want you kids to be free," he elbowed me. "But your mother wants you to conform."

For my first day of school, Mother prepared me a week in advance by gradually cutting my blankie into extinction with quilting scissors. The first few cuts were subtle. Just the decorative fringe. I figured she was making modifications so I would sneeze less. The tassels were kind of itchy. But then she went right down the center, and I found what looked like an oversized restaurant napkin on my pillow. The next day it was a sheet of paper. And finally I was snuggling with a greeting card. I figured she thought an oldest male child should do

without what could be construed by those pimply missionaries as feminine comfort, so I tossed it myself, to give her the
chance of feeling temporarily wise. "It worked wonders," she
told a sister in Oregon. "He just threw it out."

Then she assembled a homemade yellow outfit for my
first day. Half Chinese waiter, half golf caddie. The large kids
would not be lacking a dork to hurl off the monkey bars.

Dad drove me in his truck. We parked across from the
school, and he said it was completely my decision. I was in
charge. Go to school. Don't go to school. Whatever I wanted.

"I wanna go home."

He nodded for a while, then started the truck.

Mother wasn't impressed. I'd been deprived of a landmark.
My first day of school.

Dad said, "Tomorrow will be his first."

But tomorrow was the same. Rather than sit in the truck,
we went to a small asphalt playground and watched through a
rusted fence topped with barbed wire. Dad said, "Doesn't that
look fun?"

It looked like a dog pound filled with mental patients.
Kids were running and screaming and grabbing things from
each other.

A blonde girl came over to ask what we were doing.

Dad said, "My son's deciding if he wants to go to school.

Do you like it in there?"

"Yes."

"You hear that?"

The girl told me, "You get to play."

I whispered to Dad, "I don't wanna play."

He nodded longer this time, over how upset Mother would be, and she didn't disappoint. She was waiting on the porch.

They argued in the bedroom for a while, then Mother came out and gripped my arm. She led me to the front door. "You remember what brave is, honey? It's when you don't want to do something, but you do it anyway."

I was hoping Dad would step up and hit a freedom homer, but he only said, "God, don't tell him that."

✳

Mother didn't talk during the drive. She took me to a classroom doorway and motioned an elderly woman out into the corridor. She said, "I'm sorry he's late," and walked away.

"Mom?"

She didn't look back.

I figured it was a mix-up. This couldn't be it. "Mom?" There had to be some kind of misunderstanding, so I decided to yell a little. But this only prompted the old woman to grab my arm. What the hell is going on, and who is this hag pulling on me? I decided it was time to scream bloody murder and flop around like a catfish, but that was one strong hag. She held on, and Mother still wouldn't look back. She rounded the corner and disappeared. So I finally shut up.

*

Mother designs and sews most of my clothes, but nothing has zippers. To pee, I have to drop my pants and underwear to my ankles. So when three older kids came into the restroom, they saw a kid dressed like a French surrealist standing at an adult-sized urinal with his ass hanging out. Missing the first day had given Mother a chance to change my outfit. Now it was a flowery short-sleeved blouse with a nearly transparent white scarf, secured in front with what looked like a wooden napkin ring. But the big kids took care of it for me. The urinal went all the way to the floor. They taught me about zippers by pinning me in it and counting out twenty-five flushes.

*

During recess, I fell in love with the blonde girl who had talked to Dad and me through the fence. It was a horrible feeling.
She wore overalls. I wrote a note—*Can we be friends?*—and
planned to slip it into one of her overall pockets. But a little
karate expert showed up during my move. He'd been making
threatening gestures all day. He wanted everybody to know
he could kick our heads off. As I eased the note in, this random bastard planted a full-steam heel in my back, sending me
plowing into my girlfriend.

She turned to see a red-faced imbecile on the ground.
Croaking for air. Holding up a scrap of paper that she couldn't
read. None of the kids, it turned out, could read yet. She
walked away, looking irritated, and I didn't try again. My sister had taught me enough about kicking to know that it was
rarely happenstance.

❋

Mother was cuddling a bucket of fried chicken at home. I startled her, so she blew the usual shame fuse. A grimace meant to
look like a big smile. Grease like lip gloss. She set the bucket
behind her chair. Look, no chicken. No *National Enquirer* on
her lap.

Relax, Mother, I'm just coming home from my first day of school. I didn't see anything, and I don't remember what I saw.

"Congratulations, son. You're on the road to college."

My sister had already passed on everything she learned during her first years of school. When she wasn't stomping me, she tutored me. Often she combined the two. So really, since I was the only student who could read and write, I was on the road to looking out the window a lot.

Mother said, "I was just reading the news. They're saying now that eighty percent of fires are started by fire department captains."

"What?"

"They did a nationwide investigation."

"That doesn't sound right."

"It surprised me too. And it's not just firefighters. It's the captains doing it now."

"How is that possible?"

"It's true. So how was school?"

"You're telling me eighty percent of fires are started by fire captains?"

"Don't give me that look. It's true! So how was school?"

"Fine."

Mother rarely eats out in the open. But knock on her door after dinner and she shouts "Hold on!" from a throat jammed with private fudge. She refuses many family meals with the phrase "Not until I take some of this weight off."

The wording bothers Dad. "She makes it sound like she's carrying around someone else's corporate freight."

Dad thinks she's the one having the "midlife," countering his journey with a crisis of her own. Dedicating herself to the consumption of three to four times more food than necessary. If her husband is going to be dissatisfied with the life they've built, she will avenge her honor by eating everything in sight.

But she can't seem to eat enough, so she's been supplementing with pointless lying. At first, it was simply an effort to seem optimistic. If I crept in to console her, she instantly stopped blubbering. "Hi there, hon. Everything's fine." I usually went in only because nobody else seemed to notice her slinking off to cry with slabs of chocolate. When I mentioned it to Dad, he said I shouldn't worry about it. "Your mother is a victim, and that's what victims do." So I just added it to my list of chores. Go in and fix it. We love you, Mother, don't be devastated. Don't cry three times a day. I'll do the dishes and take out the trash. I'll get Dad to show respect.

But once the lying kicked in, hope was somewhat lost. Empowerment slogans—"Life is short, honey, so make it a great day!"—quickly mutated into habitual fibbing: "I had such a great day!" She has become what Dad now calls "the biggest liar on the planet, depending on how you define *intentional*."

If we ask for money, she says, "I don't have a penny," then slips the pizza man a twenty. But she also scrambles things in ways that seem involuntary. It's like that telephone game. A phrase gets whispered down a line of people, and when the final person speaks out loud, "If I had a hammer" has become "Border monkey please don't bite." Mother accomplishes this without the whispering, or the other people.

At a Mormon fellowship potluck, someone told a story about something that happened to someone's car. When Mother passed the story along five minutes later, not only did it now include several alligators, but she failed to recognize that one of the people listening was the man who had originally told the story. "Ma'am, are you insane?" is the question that nobody ever asks. But I can see that question in their eyes, and it's a misdiagnosis I'm always grateful for. Much preferable to the actual problem, which appears to be staggering stupidity.

Chapter 4

The foreman finally breaks the news in a genuine funk. "I've heard some things, Jamison. I hate to do it, but I'm cutting you loose."

"What?"

The foreman wears a colostomy bag like a purse jammed into his pants. Most of the carpenters dislike him because he wears heavy cologne to hide the odor, but Dad claims to be empathetic. "I got so upset that I couldn't use the toilet because here was this young guy trying to date with a bag on. I thought, How's this guy gonna operate? I mean, what's he gonna do? Women aren't gonna go for that, you know? So I called the doctor. I thought I had cancer or something, but he said it was probably just sympathy constipation."

The foreman tells him, "I think you've got potential, but it sounds like the other men don't necessarily see it that way."

"Who doesn't?"

He holds out an envelope. "I paid you for the full week. Go home."

"Was it that Bob bastard?"

"I'd rather not get into it. Hell, I wanted to make you foreman on another job. But it's a team effort."

"I've got a family to feed, Jerry!"

"Damn it, I know that."

Dad unlatches his carpenter's belt like he's handing in a
badge. "Christ, what am I gonna do now?"

He drives straight to a dumpster for moving boxes, but
finds something else entirely: an old man in the dumpster,
eating cold spaghetti from a dented can and grinning like a
euphoric half-wit. His face is covered with grime. His teeth
have festered down to brown spikes, but he flaunts his loot
like it's Halloween candy. Broiled chicken, broccoli, canned
artichoke hearts, a mystery novel, a bag of limes. Most of
it goes to his sixty-year-old girlfriend waiting in a nearby
park, but it's very important to share with strangers. After
eighty-six years of life, that's a valuable lesson he's learned.
It makes other people feel good, and you never know when
you'll need a favor yourself. The first one in the dumpster
has a claim, sure, and the next guy has to respect that. But
if you share something one day, and another day you find
squat, don't worry because *wham*, somebody is gonna share
with you.

He offers Dad some chicken. Plenty to go around, and just thrown out this morning. All wrapped up tight in plastic. No worse than day-old bread, and Lord knows the price is right.

Dad says no thanks, but spends the rest of the evening thinking about the coincidence. We need to cut back on expenses to facilitate a move to a fabulous ski resort, and suddenly here is a "messenger" with the solution. A sign. Chest deep in garbage, the old man seemed more relaxed and content than Dad can remember ever feeling. He tells me, "This guy was the happiest person I've seen in years!" Trashing makes money obsolete. No reason to pay for food. It waits out back, same as on the shelf. Maybe it's not as clean or spiffy, but it looks plenty tasty, and it's free. So he's free! Making a living means simply finding something edible, then the rest of the day is wide open.

✦

Dad holds up two tickets to a live Evel Knievel show. I assume they were free because I've never attended an event with Dad that required tickets. That's Mother's system: Disneyland, movies, Knott's Berry Farm. Dad prefers piers, public swimming pools, or community college weight rooms where children aren't allowed. While Dad would bodybuild, I'd slink around the gymnasium trying to avoid an irate janitor who yells gibberish—a language Dad is able to identify as "something other than English."

Dad waves the tickets. "Happy B-day." My birthday was six days ago, but I still get goose bumps because Mr. Knievel is my hero. The only man in America to break, one bad tilt at a time, "every bone in his body." And it's a good time for a little inspiration because the situation with my sister has become somewhat unbearable. I'm hoping Evel has a few pointers, facing *the dragon* as often as he does.

I even resorted recently to recruiting my little brother—an awful deal for him since he clutches his blankie almost continuously to avoid exactly the kind of combat I was trying to drag him into. He's been using his baby voice as a fist repellent, but now I was asking him to get beaten silly in the name of brotherhood only because I couldn't come up with a decent strategy of my own. He either didn't understand what I was asking, or he changed his mind mid-rush.

A diary entry in Dad's poetry book describes my brother like this:

You can't see him naked. You can't see him in his underwear even. He runs really fast. If he has his underwear on, he zips from room *to room. Super modest. They'll all be using the Slip 'N Slide, and he'll run at it like he's going to do it. But then at the last minute, he swerves away. And we all clap and cheer just like he's done it.*

This was precisely what he did during our ambush, which I concocted as revenge for a neck lashing administered by my sister with a Spiderman belt. I came from the kitchen, and my brother from the bathroom. But at the moment of impact, my brother swerved away into make-believe, leaving me to slide alone into the mouth of this shark we'd been asked to call Sister.

When I'd mastered the alphabet, my sister brandished Tonka trucks and offered me three seconds to learn how to read. She explained how little boys could never have sex once they're hit hard enough in the temple with little trucks. Sex was like a hot dog. "The man is the wiener and the woman is the bun. Now read! One . . . two . . . three!" The counting technique is what Mother uses when looking for cooperation with chores. When I turned to flee, my sister heaved the truck point-blank against the back of my skull. So reading came fast. I dashed from room to room with a Dr. Seuss while she flung trucks. Cornered on an unknown word, I danced around like a scarecrow.

She preferred me dead from day one, tipping my crib and

rolling me under a desk in the hope that newborns starve in just a few minutes. This was described by Dad. Mother has no memory of any "difficulty between the children." Dad tracked my cooing to the desk, then fastened the crib legs to the floor with drywall screws. Mother explained to my sister that they still loved her to the ends of the earth, regardless of a new male baby who would be capable of carrying on the family name. She would always be their "little sweetness pie." A few hours later, they found her ramming my soft spot with an unsharpened number-two pencil. Mother said her feelings were apparently age-appropriate, but they never subsided.

Now she steps on my toes while punching. This way, I fall backward and she can get to the fun part. The kicking. If I fight back, it worsens, so I've learned to cover up and wait patiently. This is often quite difficult, depending on the quality of shoe, but it usually works because she gets bored when there's no screeching.

Her transition from battle wrath to boredom is always a strange moment. Out of curiosity, the kicking goes on even after the rage wears off. *What hurts more, kidneys or spine? Can the actual hole of an ass be kicked, or just the cheeks? Exactly where are those infamous balls?* And it's certainly the most sensitive phase of any attack. If I glance up as she slows down, to verify an early finish, the next kick comes straight down into my teeth, and it starts all over.

A common mistake is to forget about a beating. This makes her boil. She wants very much to be remembered. She wants to be the scariest thing around. When I offered half an orange about five minutes after getting clocked in the shoulder blade with a croquet mallet, she pinned me and squeezed the orange into my eyes like acid. Then she fetched one of about four hundred hollow tipless yellow fiberglass arrow shafts, which Dad had purchased at a swap meet in case they somehow came in handy someday. They do, nearly every day. She never uses the same arrow twice, and never returns it to the main bundle. She discards it into a dim one-foot space between the garage and the fence, as if vigorous contact with skin has soiled it. A terrible pile is growing in there.

The first lash to my middle back was applied during the rinsing out of my orange eyes. I ran out the front door like a swerving blind ostrich, and she chased me to sheer exhaustion, until I sprawled on my face in a gravel alley. She's going to kill you, I informed myself. Don't watch.

But she just hovered and listened to my pathetic sobbing. She watched me wait for my trouncing, which much more satisfying than actually giving it.

What I lack is courage.

So I hope to see Evel Knievel identify failure. Just before

hitting pavement like a gas-soaked rag doll. Before writhing a hundred yards trying to kick free from a treacherous Honda stuck in full throttle. If I can see him face that moment, maybe I can understand grit. Splice together all the footage of Evel in flight, minus the launches and landings, and you won't see a superstar. You'll see an American in a silver jumpsuit, sitting in a dark sky. And he will have this to say:

"I'm afraid. But I'm still doing things."

Dad takes a shot at discussing the trash idea with Mother, without disclosing his job loss. She is mortified. How can he be envious of a homeless person? Freedom means choices, and that old man in the dumpster has none. But Dad has plenty. He should be making something of his life, instead of thinking low-class thoughts.

"Huh?" Dad is busy with more low-class thoughts, which drag him into the bedroom. They suggest he bring along a pocketknife.

He uses the knife to carve "Aark" into a leather belt, then comes out wearing the belt around his stomach. He's too excited to thread it through his belt loops. He gets our attention and makes this announcement:

"This is who I really am. Nice to meet you. I'm Aark, the Heathen Scavenger."

Then he goes out the front door.

Mother looks at me and gives a long shrug. "I don't know what he's talking about. I don't know what he means. Where's he going? Do you know what he's talking about?" And so on.

Chapter 5

Mother carries none of the fat in her face. Talking over a fence, she looks normal-sized, but then she tries to walk and her joints scream. Carrying the weight of an extra person has taken a toll on her knees. "When I go up stairs, it's like somebody's riding piggyback." What always sounded like noisy flooring has turned out to be catastrophic damage to knee cartilage. It has ground to nothing, which allows her flagrant use of the phrase "bone on bone." An actual medical term, it turns out. I was hoping the knee surgeon would make use of the phrase "Don't be ridiculous, ma'am." But he says instead, pointing to Mother's X-ray with what looks like a conductor's wand, "See here, there's nothing. It's bone on bone."

The surgeon has questions for Mother regarding rehabilitation, which will require extensive self-discipline. But with each question, he glances at me first, as if gauging something.

"You can ask anybody," Mother says. "I've never had a shortage of discipline."

The surgeon stares at me, as if waiting for some high sign.

"OK. Well, we need to do a physical before we can schedule anything."

On our way to the nurses' station, Mother goes pale in the hallway. "I shouldn't feel so nervous. I'm a real self-sufficient person."

I tell her, "People feel nervous all the time."

"Thank you, honey, it's nice of you to say that. It's just that they cut your leg completely off during the operation." She teeters and braces herself against a wall, pouring sweat. "I guess that's what's bothering me."

"What?" I help her sit on a gurney next to a bathroom door.

"Yeah, they cut your leg off and set it aside." She tips over and passes out.

A nurse rushes over to mop her forehead. "Ma'am, can you hear me? Are you on any medication?"

I say, "I think she's scared."

"No," Mother mumbles, "I'm not scared. I just didn't eat. I should've eaten."

＊

Because of Mother's massive arms, the blood pressure cuff blows off during inflation. The nurse says, "This one's not big enough," then tears plastic from a new cuff and hooks it up. But again, the cruel drumroll scratch of Velcro. The three of us holding our breath until the cuff fails again and flops to the floor.

Mother says, "Try it on my wrist. That's what they did last time."

It works, but when the nurse leaves, Mother offers me this revision: "The Velcro was no good on those. That's the problem."

"What?"

"They were old ones. The Velcro couldn't hold."

I find myself gazing into space as the surgeon comes in.

This is a new twist. Mother usually fibs only when there are no obvious witnesses, but now she's asking me to consent. The nurse did not open a brand-new cuff. She did not say the first one was too small, and I am not sitting right here with human ears.

The surgeon says nothing can be done until significant weight is lost. Mother asks about stinging herself with honeybees in the meantime.

"Pardon me?"

"My husband does it. You sting where there's arthritis and it draws the body's natural cortisone to the area."

"The body doesn't have natural cortisone."

"Well, it works wonders for my husband. He's been doing

it for years. The pain goes away for months at a time."

The surgeon nods a while, "Hmm," then writes a number on an index card and hands it to Mother. It's how many pounds she must lose before an operation can be scheduled. Then he shakes my hand good-bye for an oddly long time, stopping only after I finally look at him. His eyes seem moist, and his eyebrows are out of control.

On the street, Mother won't show me the number. "Did you like him? I didn't like him."

✦

Dad is gathering bees from a neighbor's flowerbed down the street when Mother announces her new diet. Two weeks of only sauerkraut. She reads things and constantly drops pounds with snazzy one-food gimmicks. Chicken broth every forty-five minutes. Cantaloupe halves filled with water. The white mulch on the inside of orange peels. For five days the fridge was stacked with peeled oranges, which hardened almost instantly, but Dad wouldn't let her throw them away.

She lost fifteen pounds, then chronic gloom required her to stuff her feelings with auxiliary pastries. A month after each diet, our civilian scale is maxing out again at a smooth 250. Dad tried to make a bet with me last time. He wanted to bet

five bucks that a military or zoo scale would detect at least another forty pounds.

Dad strides ceremoniously through the living room with a
mason jar full of bees and a sandwich bag of ice cubes. Mother
has agreed to the procedure on one condition. It has to oc-
cur somewhere "the children can't see." Dad offers us a look
of mock sincerity, then a wink, and leaves the master bedroom
door ajar so we can watch in stacked silence.

A book called *Bees Don't Get Arthritis* got Dad started. But
he doesn't just sting arthritic joints. He stings moles and flaky
skin. Corns on his feet. A blotch on his forehead where he
thought skin cancer might be brewing. He stung what he calls
the gap, a spot just below the pubic bone, centimeters above
wiener. He says it carries mystic Eastern significance. He
hoped a little bee poison might get his "metaphysical juices
flowing." All it did was double him over for ten minutes.

Mother is on the bed, facing the wall. She says it again.
"They cut your leg off completely during the surgery. I think
that's what's bothering me."

Dad says, "Wrong."

"I read it. They cut it off and set it aside."

"Christ."

"Why do you think that's not true?"

"Because it doesn't make any sense! Why would they do

that?"

"I read it."

"Horseshit."

"It's true."

Dad tugs her stretch pants down below the knees, rather than roll one pant leg up. Mother rarely wears panties because she prefers "pretty ones," which require a special order from Sprouse-Ritz. And according to Dad, she resents having to confess to teenaged clerks, "Super double-assed, please."

Dad is classy enough to numb her dimpled flesh with ice, but it's too much for me. As the first bee catches skin, Mother groans with such vulgar submission that I run, the vastness of butt crack having brought on an uncontrollable snicker, which turns into a sneezing frenzy over Mother's reproductive area resembling an uncooked calzone with wildly long hair plugs.

My brother and sister find me afterward to offer a detailed report, so it's necessary to run some more.

The bees work, though.

＊

Dad comes at me next, the hum of the infuriated bees amplified by the glass jar. He pretends it's a test to determine whether I'm allergic, but really he just hates to waste bees. A son named Paul from his first marriage was allergic without knowing. He found this out in a Mexican jungle, where Dad had moved our family for an agonizing six-month campout to prove that people could still be carefree and adventurous after having three children. Paul drove down on a motorcycle and got stung next to a river, then immediately started choking on his bloated tongue.

We all ran hysterical circle-eights back and forth from the tent to the truck while Paul fell on the ground wheezing. We were looking for the first-aid kit, which nobody had packed, and which held no antidote anyway.

Paul's tongue eventually shrunk on its own.

So Dad wants to know in advance this time, but he considers the $8.99 pouch of epinephrine unnecessary. He researched exactly which drugstore shelf it is on, and his truck is idling outside, ready for a quick rescue.

Mother says, "Why don't you buy the antidote and take it back if he doesn't need it?"

"I've got it figured out. Can you just leave us alone?"

I close my eyes and take the bee on my arm. It *must* be an allergic reaction. Half my body is immediately engulfed in flame. I start howling.

"Come on, now," Dad says. "That's only one!" His formula is six bees per square inch of pain.

I jump around a little. "I'm allergic!"

"No, just relax a second." He usually presses on the poison
sac attached to the stinger, in order to get every drop of good-
ness. But I can't take it. I pinch the stinger out, and the scorch-
ing dies down.

"Well, look at that," he says. "You're a mainliner." He has
stung directly into the artery bulging in the crook of my el-
bow. "Shit, no wonder you're yelling so much. It went straight
to your heart probably."

Chapter 6

Wearing his hand-carved Aark belt, Dad cruises behind local grocery stores, then parks to wait at the original dumpster in hopes of spotting the Messenger. He wants to pick the old man's brain for secrets of the trade. When a box-boy carries out a gallon jar of pickled eggs under his arm like a football, Dad picks his own brain.

The passage from *in* to *out* is simple capitalist magic. Nothing about the eggs has changed. A minute earlier they cost good money. Now they're free, but instantly transformed into pig slop by new scenery. Top shelf, bottom shelf, discount rack, back alley. American food products are being priced according to location.

Dad peeks over the edge of the bin. There's a split-open fifty-pound bag of dry dog food. Perfect initiation. He can test the water without putting anything in his mouth. Do it for Buffy, our loyal family dog. Save the five dollars her food costs every week. A few minutes in the dumpster would equal five smackers. That's close to a hundred dollars an hour. Best job in the world! He could return home with mildew fur growing on his forearms, and at a hundred per, even Mother can't nag.

He climbs in for the dog food, then spots the pickled eggs. The jar is clean. Expiration date only one day past. The lid? Snug. So he pops it off, the dumpster suddenly feeling like half foxhole, half gold mine. He hesitates only long enough to sniff the top egg, then wolfs it. Delicious! The jar will feed his family for days, and "trash" isn't just edible. The word itself is a subliminal allspice.

He races home and hands each of us one covert egg, trembling. "Can you believe how good these are?"

Mother agrees after a third egg, allowing her mouth the necessary warm-up. She hasn't yet noticed the black felt-tip X marked on the lid of the jar.

❋

Evel is scheduled to jump ten big rigs. I expect them to be end-on-end, rather than side-by-side, but really the trucks are insignificant. He could jump a long sandbox. It's his willingness to spend *any* time airborne, after so many inhuman spills, that matters. The opening act is two hours of explosive drag racing and funny-car parades. The announcer screams about how over the top they are. Then Evel spends half an hour doing bleacher-length wheelies, standing on his seat or no-hands style.

When he finally jumps, I can't see a goddamn thing. Every camera flash in the opposite bleacher goes off at once, leaving me with only my little prayer: "Please, crash."

I don't want him injured, but a successful jump means nothing. He has to bite it and walk away. Badly banged but not discouraged. If I can harness that kind of nerve during my daily stompings, my sister won't stand a chance. She can't win unless I lose. It's impossible to overpower her. She's built like a brick hate house. But maybe I can underpower her. A bloody mouth doesn't matter so much. She's more interested in demoralizing fright. She wants your pants to fill with brown human terror. Learn to deny her this, and she will become categorically bored. I will just rise up. And up again. "Thank you, sir, may I have another!"

But Evel doesn't crash. It is reportedly a gorgeous landing.

✳

Mother meets us at the front door, pointing to the X on the lid of the pickled egg jar. "This better not mean what I think it means, so help me God!"

Dad opens his mouth to deny it, but freezes mid-epiphany. He decides what the hell. He'll be himself. Even if nobody wants him to. "Yeah . . . it's trash. And I lost my stupid job."

Mother staggers to her room.

Dad follows her.

I immediately charge my sister, arms flailing to appear beside myself. A vicious orangutan. Evel's skillful landing planted the notion of offense, and a ridiculous feeling of invincibility. I somehow momentarily forget that nothing on God's green earth frightens her.

She shuts down my lungs with a fist rifled into my guts. I try to rise up and ask for another, but there's a distinct lack of air. I'm arching on the floor and gasping for wonderful oxygen. I very much want to be someone who can fight impressively without concern for his body. A fight to the death. But then what? Even if I miraculously survive, I'll still be myself. Pain will still hurt. Pretending will change nothing. My noncourage is a hard fact, and practice will not make perfect. So I just roll around on the carpet and wait for my lungs to start working again.

In the bedroom, Dad offers Mother details of Bob scrambling from the shitter of a Sambo's restaurant. Pale as a ghost. Bob had been doing his thing—straining, surrounded by festive tile and that chemical stench—when he suddenly felt out-and-out fear. "What if I fucking die in here?!"

Now Dad finally understands what he meant, and he wants to punch himself in the face for taking so long. He's been working for new furniture, shoes, and goddamn magazine subscriptions. Making petty routines a priority. He's handed authority over to some persona—who he should be, instead of who he is. But those eggs are undeniable. More trash means less work. Less work means more time. And finally, more life! Think of it! We can do whatever the hell we want! No work. Just skiing, sledding, igloo building. Food stamps.

No! Mother despises food stamps. People snicker in grocery lines and checkers are condescending. She wants a normal, above-board life. Her father raised ten children and never once resorted to crummy welfare or scavenging. She wants to move to Oregon instead and be near Mormons who cherish her. Dad can hang drywall with her tall brother and ski on the weekends.

"You're missing the point," Dad says. "I don't want to waste *any* more days. None."

Mother smothers herself with a pillow and blurts, "I won't do it!"

Dad comforts her. "There, there."

Then he finds us on the front porch and offers more eggs. He sits to describe an African snake he saw on a National Geographic television program. "The two-step something. It bites you, you take two steps, and you're dead. That's how we oughta live. The snake just nailed us. We've only got two steps. So make 'em good, huh?"

In ten days, we will leave for Mammoth Mountain, California.

Part Two

Mammoth Lakes, California, 1975

Chapter 7

We rent an A-frame house in Mammoth for two-fifty per month, just a few miles below some thirty ski lifts. As we unpack, a fish hatchery truck beeps down our driveway to stock the creek behind our house with rainbow trout.

Dad says, "Talk about a good omen!"

We don't bother with fishing poles. The creek is churning, so we blitz the freezing water to grope. It's my first fish. Fourteen inches long, grabbed with cold bare hands. I raise it up over my head, and we're all yelling.

My sister wants to keep the fish. She names it Norton and starts filling the bathtub. But I'm so excited, I inadvertently throttle her new pet to death. It goes belly up in the tub. Mashed in the middle, eyes bulging.

Dad gives it a proper burial in the oven, then gathers us for our first meal in our new house, surrounded by Christmas trees oozing sap that smells like vanilla. He lights fat, lopsided, half-melted candles from a dumpster. My sister refuses her portion as Dad passes out plates of flaky Norton.

＊

At our first bin, the thought of someone seeing us (of Mother seeing us) just about stops my heart, so I stand back while my sister and brother help Dad transfer food to the truck.

Dad is beside himself. He yells "Jackpot!" and waves celery in the air, then cinnamon graham crackers. He's never this manic at home, so I take it as a glimpse of his real self. Deliriously happy on the inside, but lacking a good enough reason to ever show it. He tosses me a smashed box of Cocoa Puffs—my favorite cereal—and it happens. He asks, "What are you waiting for?" to tip the scale, and I climb in.

Dad credits the strange solace of getting something for nothing, but it's just the sensation of finally being *with* him. The actual father. This feeling weighs more than the disgrace.

I expect maggots and blinding stench, but it's more like an outdoor discount rack. Dented cans of sweet potato. Candy bars looking like someone stepped on them just a little. And so much. A rack of papayas ripe enough to burst. Cookie boxes with broken corners, which dooms the cookies even though they're wrapped in plastic. A crate of onion-flavored potato chips, day-old bagels, a dozen jumbo peach yogurts.

Dad is thrilled because the local economy is tourist driven, and skiers want perfect food. The instant a piece of fruit shows age, it gets ditched. When a manager needs shelf space for granola bars and trail mix, he abandons items that aren't selling. "Looks like we picked the right town for trashing!"

Finding enough to feed a family of five will be a breeze. Getting Mother on board might not be.

✦

Dad rehearses what to tell Mother about a truck bed full of secondhand food. Free stuff is satisfying because it's a gift from something intangible. No strings attached. The world is handing out treats. Our only task is to reach up and pick fruit from friendly trees. "Some people feel that they have to work in order to deserve things, that you have to earn what you get. But that's just social conditioning. Then there's no finding. When you find a dollar on the street, it seems very pungent, right? What a meaningful thing that is. . . ."

Mother isn't home. We deliver the groceries, but not too many of any one item. That would look suspect. And only the least damaged packages. There are eighteen chicken potpies, but they all have an X. Dad transfers seven of them into aluminum foil. "We'll tell her it's because they freeze better in foil."

The truck is still half full, so we go back to the dumpster.

Dad turns over boxes to use as display tables for all the extra. "For the next guy." It looks like an abandoned yard sale.

*

We park next to the ski lodge to watch paying customers use the rope tow. There's a ton of snow, but the sun is shining. I see several skiers wearing only T-shirts. Dad doesn't have enough money for lift tickets. His plan is to save up unemployment checks for a season pass. My sister and brother are gorging on candy bars. I'm worried that once you eat garbage, you can't go back. You're a different person. But candy is candy, and I'm starving, so I choose the least crushed Snickers bar from a box of about twenty. Dad notices me staring at it and says this:

"People get upset about trash because they don't know how to trust. They're afraid to eat what they find because they think nature has some kind of savage agenda. They see a rabbit get killed by a wolf on TV and they call it conflict, but it's actually cooperation. The rabbit isn't running from the wolf, it's running with the wolf. The chase is just this dance. When people wish the rabbit could escape, what they're really wishing is that it wasn't a rabbit at all. Probably because they don't want to feel like that damn rabbit does. So they pretend they can escape nature. They try to distance themselves by wearing fancy clothes and driving nice cars."

I put the Snickers back in the box so that Dad won't think
he can talk me into something. He nods a moment, bothered,
then starts the truck and drives to an isolated hill on the fringe
of the ski area. One face of the hill is clear of trees.

My brother says, "I have a stomachache."

"Just remember," Dad says, "when people see the world
as unfriendly, they deflate their natural space. They learn to
struggle, instead of just reaching up to pick the fruit that's
waiting for them. They're afraid the tree might be bare. And
according to what they think they need, it probably is. So they
dig ditches for money, or become a carpenter. Then they pay
someone else to pick their fruit."

"My stomach hurts."

"If we were on a beach, we'd be spearing fish and eating
from that environment. Or in the forest, we'd gather mush-
rooms or some kind of critter. But the city offers us the dumpster, so that is where we'll make our living. We can get food in
just a few minutes, with very little effort, and have fun digging
around. Then we have the whole day to play. We could work,
work, work, and we'd get money for that, but how much does
it cost to buy back one day?"

"Dad?"

"No amount of money . . ." He jumps out and starts jacking up the back of the truck. He swaps the tire for a bare wheel, then carries another wheel up the hill and secures it over a low broken branch. A rope goes around both bare wheels and the ends get spliced together.

I ask, "What are you doing?"

"The differential on this truck isn't positraction, which means only the lifted wheel turns."

"What?"

"You'll see."

The back of the truck is filled with mismatched ski gear. At a flea market we stuffed grocery sacks full for one dollar each. Down jackets, mittens, wool socks. Skis with bindings were five dollars. Nothing matched, but Dad said it was cool to have different-colored ski boots. He told us to buy two right-handed gloves, then wear one backward. All the skis were too long for us, so he picked ones with logos behind the bindings, then cut them in half with a hacksaw and reattached the bindings in the new middles.

He wedges a brick against the gas pedal to keep the wheel going, but the rope is too loose. It spins free over the thrustwheel when we grip. Dad tightens it with loop knots, which thump each time they pass over the wheels. But now we have something to grab. One at a time, we go up the hill. We have our own rope tow.

My brother is afraid, so Dad stands him on the front of his skis and they go down the hill together.

The paying skiers are starting to head home. They slow down to figure out what the hell we're doing. Soon there's a small traffic jam with congratulatory honking. One car pulls over for quite a while to watch. The man finally taps his horn and rolls down his window. "My God, I thought I was crazy about fishing!"

Chapter 8

Mother tilts a box of Cheerios, but Honeycombs pour out.
She stares at the bowl, then at her children around the table
holding our breath. Dad asked us to take down cereal boxes
and top them off with Honeycombs from a crushed box. He
said we should start stockpiling cartons and wrappers from
food that Mother bought. We can use them as disguises.
"That's really all she's buying anyway. The containers."

Mother starts to say something, then sort of winces instead. "That's a good one." She sniffs the milk before pouring
it. "You kids are funny."

*

Dad has spent the morning in his lawn chair, thinking hard
about something. When Mother finally goes out there, I hide
at the corner of the porch to listen. It's cold, but she hasn't
bothered with a coat because conversation between them is
always brief and unpleasant. The insides of her legs rub as she

crosses the yard. All her pants are blue or brown polyester and stretch to whatever size she needs.

Cancer has sprouted in the uterus of our dog, Buffy.

Dad got the diagnosis before leaving Huntington Beach. The veterinarian was optimistic because the tumor is isolated, and it's a common procedure. Just eliminate the female parts. But Dad is uncomfortable. It seems unnatural to him, and vets are worse crooks than mechanics.

"She's not a car," Mother says. "Just take her in."

"I don't know. . . ."

"Use the Christmas money if you have to. The kids won't mind."

"Christmas money?"

"The money I gave you. Just use that."

"That was for Christmas?"

"Did you spend it?"

Dad turns his head and works his hands together—a gesture he's been perfecting for years. It's meant to suggest that his thoughts are more interesting than Mother's words. "No."

"OK, so use that." Mother hugs herself. "I'm cold."

"OK."

"I'm going in."

"OK."

I crouch down as she makes the porch planks groan. Then Buffy comes out from under the house, as if to fill the space Mother left. She sits next to Dad and wags her crooked tail, which stayed bent after a car taught her to keep off the road by bouncing her off. Dad doesn't pet her. He just rests his hand on her skull. When Buffy opens her mouth to pant, wearing the hand like a cap, it looks like she's smiling.

＊

After their first shopping trip together, Mother sends herself to her room. She was headed for the automatic doors, clutching those dreaded food stamps, when Dad veered off around the side of the market—"The adventure's in back, babe!"

Dad claims she's upset because his groceries were in boxes instead of paper bags. "Your mother is horrified. She says she doesn't want to raise you kids with these low values. So we'll just have to ignore her, I guess. What else can we do?"

"I thought we weren't going to tell her."

"Yeah, I changed my mind about that."

＊

A handmade quilt is pulled over Mother's head.

I sit on the edge of the bed. "Dad says you're upset about the groceries."

"Oh, I don't want to bring you kids into it. To him it's a wonderful freedom or something. I don't understand it. To me it's shameful. You can get salmonella from your own kitchen, so what in God's world can you get from food in the dumpster that's been rotted with insects all through it?"

She lowers the quilt. "I feel it's important to give you kids a good example on how to live. I feel like your father is giving you the poorest example he can. It's embarrassing to me. I actually didn't understand what he was doing at first. I thought maybe there was a vendor parked behind the market. But then I saw this look on his face and it finally dawned on me. I realized what he was doing. Very repulsive to me, as you can imagine. Someone who is supposed to be your companion for life. I've lost a lot of respect for him. A tremendous amount of respect."

I stand up to leave.

"You just gave me an idea."

"What?"

"Nothing. Thank you for coming in. I got an idea. I don't know what I'd do without you."

"What?"

*

Her idea is to go on strike. She announces that she won't speak again until her children are garbage-free. Not a word, and not a single chore.

Dad celebrates by bringing down a sourdough culture thriving in a pint jar above the stove. He mixes it into Bisquick from a torn box to make towering stacks of pancakes that he calls "gooners." Smothered with coconut syrup from behind the health food store.

Mother has unintentionally put him in charge of food.

"Who wants gooners?!"

"Me!"

"Me!"

"Me!"

Chapter 9

Mother switches to a hunger strike. The sauerkraut didn't work anyway. Now it's only water. We see her three times the first day—stomping to the bathroom with a romance novel. The jackets of her books always feature people about to copulate on a jagged cliff in high winds, or in a meadow with a chuck wagon and a loose horse in the background. The bathroom wall is simply a quarter-inch-thick sheet of plywood painted white, so the sound of her urine stream fills the house. Then back to her bedroom with another pitcher of ice water.

By the second day, Dad has packed the refrigerator. When Mother opens the freezer for ice, TV dinners tumble out. From the fridge, it's a landslide of Hostess fruit pies. So she declares the fridge off limits.

Dad finds an abandoned fridge in an alley and installs it next to the water heater. He declares his fridge off limits to her.

Mother bans trashing at her favorite store.

Dad bans shopping at his favorite. He hides desserts under our pillows while we sleep.

Mother finds licked-clean pudding cartons in our beds, then forbids us to eat "that!"

Dad picks us up from school to hit candy stores and pastry shops on the sly. My sister finds a variation on Twinkies—six jumbo boxes designed to be worn like backpacks. She says "Jackpot!" and runs at top speed with a tube of decorative crepe paper, flailing her arms and making a giant circle around the dumpster. The red paper unravels behind her like a parade streamer.

✦

Since neither of them broke the cancer news, I've been half-hoping that I overheard wrong. But then Dad leaves Mother a note as part of the strike negotiations. Buffy's operation has been "postponed pending further consideration. All available funds earmarked for ski pass."

And Buffy does something to prove not only that the cancer is real, but that it may have spread to her brain. She attacks a young girl.

It's a new friend of my sister's, who is helping my sister throw rocks at me. I hide first behind my little brother, but that doesn't stop them. So I crouch behind Buffy because nobody wants to hurt a dog. But the rocks keep coming, and Buffy does a lunge-and-sprint, easily snapping her chain.

It's the first time I've seen fear in my sister's eyes. She freezes with a nauseated frown and a handful of rocks held forward to deflect a charging German shepherd. But Buffy loves her. Unfortunately, the neck that gets seized does not belong to my sister.

Buffy drives the girl to the ground, then lets go and slinks to her doghouse, showing instant regret.

The girl jumps up, too stunned to cry, with a pair of deep puncture marks on each side of her windpipe. A dry vampire bite. She doesn't know what to do, and neither do we. Then the blood starts.

It doesn't squirt. It pours. The girl touches her neck and looks at her fingers. The blood tells her what to do. She screams her guts out.

Dad's first move is to pull Buffy from the doghouse in order to hit her three times in the face with an open hand. Then he motions for us to take over. He puts the screaming girl in his truck as we pile onto Buffy. But we don't use open hands. We use fists. And it goes on for quite a while.

Buffy bit me at age five and there was no punishment, but now she has violenced someone outside the family, and this somehow makes all the difference. We are a mob. Not just fists. We stomp ribs and pull her ears. My sister lifts a piece of firewood kindling to use as a club, and it somehow doesn't seem excessive.

＊

During the 1930s, next to railroad tracks in a slum of Chicago, Dad would tie a string to a chunk of raw liver and lower it into a creek. Stupid crawfish would latch on and not let go until they broke the surface of the water, which was too late. Dad would fill a bucket with crawfish for his grandmother to boil for dinner. The lump of liver was usually still dangling from the string. So he made a habit of letting his dog swallow it. "I named my dog Admiral. But I called him Pig."

When the chunk of liver was settled nice and deep, Dad would slowly reel it back up. "He always got this really weird look on his face. . . ."

His mother had moved from Chicago without him. She left him and his dog at his grandparents' house, the crawl space of which was occupied by countless wild kittens. Dad was six. He coaxed a kitten out and tried to pick it up.

"It tore my hands all to shit. I really wanted to hold it. It drove me crazy that I couldn't pick the son of a bitch up. So I got a two-by-four and snuck up on him while he was sunning himself, and Whammo! He staggered around a while until he regained his composure. I wanted to *have* him, I guess. So, I don't know. My grandparents didn't like me too much. It wasn't such a good deal. Me living there."

Then his grandfather found him hanging from a tree one afternoon, feet paddling six inches off the ground. Just in time. Dad had rigged a noose and put it around his neck, out of curiosity.

"I was pretty young, so I didn't really know what I was doing. But at the same time, I'd seen a lot of Western movies, so I knew what it meant to get hanged. And it was at a real stressful time for me, so I don't know whether to call it an accident. I mean, I was finally realizing that my parents maybe didn't care too much about me, which makes it sort of hard to care yourself."

✱

Mother steps out in a white robe with nap creases in her cheeks to interrupt our attack on Buffy. "My God! What the hell are you kids doing?"

"She bit Carol."

"So what! You can't do that to a pregnant dog!"

"What?"

"Come here, Buffy. Poor girl."

Chapter 10

Certain beatings I can't help but take seriously. For these, I reserve a special shriek—meant to either startle my sister or alert Dad. My sister is rarely startled, but every so often Dad bursts through the door and grabs the nearest item. Shoe, cassette tape, coin purse. He heaves it, knowing that my sister means business. He doesn't want to waste time crossing the room because those last few criminal kicks to my brain stem might actually finish me off.

Usually he aims loosely, but this time he nails my sister, then feels terrible. He apologizes and tries to hug her, which is impossible. She allows herself to be carried to bed, but it will be weeks before she speaks to him again.

Just stand up for yourself, I think, then Dad won't be forced to pitch wooden slingshots against his daughter's forehead.

But this will no longer be an issue, my sister explains. She has learned her lesson. She will never again beat me like a red-headed stepchild in plain sight for absolutely no reason. It will now be a long series of unfortunate accidents.

*

Dad ties a rope to the ceiling so we can swing like Tarzans. But it's an A-frame house, so be careful of the beams. My first time up, I look down to see my sister floating out of nowhere, grinning alongside two girls from the neighborhood. One is Carol with a bandaged neck. Her doctor bill was eighty dollars, and her parents were surprisingly forgiving about a vicious dog attack. They said she'd been bitten before.

My sister takes hold of the rope with both hands and makes like she's stirring a giant upside-down bowl of cookie dough. I swing in wider and wider circles until my face meets one of the diagonal beams. I drop twelve feet to the floor and black out, then almost vomit. My sister and the girls are laughing. To shut them up, I show my hands filled with blood, and they run out of the house screaming.

Then I go looking for Mother, drenched in blood now, so she screams too. She tries to pick me up, but immediately starts hyperventilating. She pulls me into the bathroom, where we both almost pass out in front of the mirror. It's like a horror movie. A jagged gash just below my eye, and a full blood beard. Mother braces herself against the wall. To calm her down, I tell her it doesn't hurt.

"I know it does, honey! I'll fix it!"

"No, I said it *doesn't* hurt."

She staggers and plops on the toilet. "Just hang in there!"

Dad shows up to call it a "blunt-force wound." Nothing sharp to break the skin. It was torn by the force of the blow. He rinses my face to study the wound, and decides to take care of it himself.

They argue quietly. My eye is swelling shut, and I seem to be contracting lockjaw.

Mother is concerned about infection.

Dad asks her not to be ridiculous. "He's more likely to get an infection at a stinking hospital than here."

Mother is worried about when the pain kicks in.

Dad takes down a bottle of aspirin and shakes it. "Since it's not a clean cut, seeing a doctor won't do any good. It'll leave a scar either way, so I might as well do it myself."

I ask, "Do what?"

Dad kneels and starts digging around in the cabinet.

I ask Mother, "Do what himself?"

She shakes her head and whispers, "Cheap bastard."

✸

Dad's father came home one night with his ear torn halfway off. Dad was fourteen. His father was a junkie named Orville. He shook Dad awake and asked him to sew the ear back on with the normal needle and thread. Dad claims to have done a pretty good job. Orville felt no pain. The chemicals in his blood saw to that.

The next morning, Orville connected a rubber tube to the exhaust pipe of his truck and closed the garage door. He got behind the wheel and started the engine, then quickly tied his own hands behind his back, in case he changed his mind during the crucial moments. He had worked on ships in the Navy. He was a knot expert.

Dad noticed a scrap of paper on the table during breakfast. It was a good-bye note. He read it, then handed it to his mother.

The note was brief:

Don't go in the garage.

✦

Dad changes his mind when it's time to push the needle into my cheek. He can't do it. He drives to a drugstore for butterfly bandages instead.

Mother blends me a milkshake for dinner because my jaw won't open. She asks my sister to present the shake to show how sorry she is, but she's the opposite of sorry. I've never heard her apologize to anybody. She once walked three miles to school for a week because she refused to apologize to the bus driver for throwing a ball of paper into the back of his head.

She can't help but grin while handing me the shake. "Hurt?"

No, goddamn it.

Dad applies the butterfly bandage—designed to let a wound breathe while pulling the edges tight. He also bought a bottle of vitamin E oil to help the scar heal. I should rub a little on every day.

I fall asleep on the couch and dream that my sister has popped my eyes out. They're on the floor, but I can still see through them. I look up at her, then at my own empty eye sockets. If our parents find my eyeballs, they'll ask her to apologize. So she picks them up and eats them. I expect them to be crunchy, but they gush like tomatoes.

Chapter 11

The night Dad finally gets his season pass, it snows three feet. He wakes us up with "Holy hell! Three feet in one night. I didn't know that was possible!" He decides to commemorate by shaving his head. Cut down on wind resistance. My sister and brother love the idea, but Mother storms out the front door wearing only a robe and holding a patch of embroidery.

She's doing embroidery at six in the morning to keep her hands busy. She never stops moving her toes. My sister once brought home a kitten that kept mistaking Mother's toes for mice and attacking them, so Mother put the kitten in a closet. When I came home, the kitten was yowling. I said, "Why don't you put shoes on?"

"What?"

"Why don't you just put shoes on?"

"Good idea."

Dad goes to the front door and gives a smile that says *Look at your silly mother, trudging through three beautiful feet of snow like an ox.* I expect him to lock her out, the way my sister usually does me, but he follows her.

My brother gets dressed and steps out onto the second-story balcony. He jumps without a moment's hesitation. The same little brother who saves most of his Halloween candy until the following Halloween. Tall fuzzy blond hair. We look down at a deep snow angel, minus the wings. His hat flew off. It's sitting beside the impression. We yell down, and he yells something back. We can't make it out, but he's giggling. My sister goes next.

I go to the bathroom to hide the electric razor. My plan is to stop Dad while convincing him that he could be bald if he really wanted to. Mother loves him regardless. Then I will convince Mother that Dad isn't being mean. He just needs to express himself with extremes. I stuff the razor into the hamper, under Mother's massive red long underwear.

Old-growth pines around our house drop cones from so high that catching one on the head, even with a wool cap, would mean damage. So when a cone slams down next to Mother, with her husband pursuing her in slow motion around the house, she takes it as a sign from the Mormon God and plows back inside.

She gathers us together, out of breath, for a family prayer. Her feet are glowing red. She thanks her Heavenly Father for sparing her, but wants to know what he meant by throwing down such a dangerous cone.

Dad stamps his boots clear and mumbles disgust over our kneeling.

Mother prays louder. "I bear my testimony that I know this church is true, and that Joseph Smith is the true prophet."

Dad heads for the bathroom. "Jesus Christ . . ."

Mother's eyes are shut tight, asking for the wisdom to protect her children from garbage. Her husband is immune because selfishness has made him thick-skinned, but her children are angelic and frail. They might suffocate on the stink, or slip and crack their heads, then drown in dumpster sludge.

Dad shouts from the bathroom, "OK, where's the electric razor?"

"I've tried to ignore him, Lord. But the more I do, the more he brings it out in the open. To the point where now he's broadcasting it even to my brothers and sisters. He's broadcasting it to everybody. I don't understand. I mean, how can someone not have enough pride that they wouldn't want people not to know. I can't believe he wants people to know! I'm very concerned that I've chosen a father for my children who wants to give them such a bad example. Amen."

"Goddamn kids!" Dad slams the bathroom door and does the job with a straight razor. It takes fifteen minutes. He appears in the doorway with a gleaming head, grinning like a dolphin.

My sister and brother are ecstatic, whooping.

Dad stands over Mother and waits for a response, but she refuses to look. She concentrates on her embroidery.

I find myself collapsing onto the sofa and crying like a stupid baby into a cushion.

"What is it?" Dad asks. "What's the matter with you?"

I have no idea.

✦

Dad shows up shirtless on the beginner slope. He is tan and glad to see me. He's glad to see anybody, having gotten lost making his own trail down the back of the mountain. "Come try the Cornice."

I follow him into the same gondola featured in that brochure back in Huntington Beach. It's like a day at the beach. Several women are in bikini tops. We can see June Lake. It's a stunning ride up, but then we stand looking over that treacherous cliff, and I realize there's a good chance I'm going to break every bone in my body. People are flying off. One guy goes right across the top of my skis, out over a lane of huge rocks, then disappears.

Dad says, "It's a pretty good drop. Just take your time and pick your route."

I edge down a little, picking my route, and instantly lose control. Head over heels. I'm worried about clacking skis and poles stabbing my eyes, until momentum tears away all equipment. Now it's just a matter of not snapping off limbs. I ball up and try to maintain one position. Still way too fast, but at least I'm on my stomach, looking over to see Dad, who's been skiing alongside me the whole time. "Attaboy!"

There's clapping nearby when I finally stop. I assume it's drop-your-lunch-tray-in-the-cafeteria applause, but a guy who carried down one of my skis says, "You're the smallest kid I've ever seen up this high."

One piece at a time, skiers bring down my equipment. I even lost a glove. My goggles are cracked, but people are telling me I'm a brave little son of a bitch. It's not bad. I tell Dad, "Let's go again."

We go six more times, until finally Dad gets tired of gathering up my trail of gear.

✳

The Cornice experience comes in handy during a school-sponsored ski race. I finally learned what my sister has been trying to teach me. Physical pain is relatively temporary.

The race is more like an obstacle course. There are poles to avoid like normal slalom, but then a tractor tire half-buried in the snow. You have to lie back and slide through without scraping your face off. Construction cones to straddle. Bales of hay, which I don't understand, and so on. But the real kicker is a huge ramp just before the finish line. This is what does in all the kids who've been skiing since they could walk. It sends the first few contestants so high, they seem to be dropping from lodge windows.

Most of the kids know just how dangerous a jump like that is, so they take it easy and look for a nice landing. But they all come down on their backs, then walk the last few yards to the finish line.

I've never taken a jump like that, so I go full blast. When the woman presses the big stopwatch to record my time, she's looking *up*.

Look at me, Mr. Knievel. An American in a silver ski suit. Upside-down in a bright sky. I'm afraid, but I'm still doing things.

I crash miserably, but *past* the finish line. Word spreads quick. The new kid has won, and not just for his age group. He's beaten everybody. A boy with prescription goggles doesn't know I'm the new kid. He says, "Some nonlocal thinks he won, but the timer is screwed up. It doesn't count."

At the awards ceremony, the principal calls my name from a podium. On my way up, somebody shouts, "Good job, Cindy!" because of my shiny red Fonzie jacket that Mother sewed from a kind of synthetic rubber-poly blend. The buttons are tiny mirrors. After my first day in that jacket, my nickname permanently became Cindy.

The principal hands me a golden trophy and says, "Congratulations, son." He shakes my hand. It's not bad.

Chapter 12

Dad wakes me up at three A.M. to assist in the carnage. The first eleven pups have monster heads and stump legs. Dad pulls them out one at a time, slimy and dead, then hands them to me. They're steaming hot. My job is to lay them carefully in the trash can. If I tilt them, blood rushes from their mouths. Buffy is upset. She seems to think we're killing her pups. Only the last one is alive, and he's blond. Dad doesn't say anything when it's over. He goes back to sleep. I sit on the back porch to watch the pup suckle next to the trash can. I tell myself this:

Look what you did.

I know.

✦

Buffy gives birth every year because Dad doesn't approve of neutering. "People change the natural order just for convenience, which is a stupid thing." It's usually a pup from the year before that gets the next litter going. But this time it was a monstrous Saint Bernard.

Dad saw Buffy getting "what for," so he carried out a two-by-four and took a full lumberjack swing down onto the Saint Bernard's head. The dog slept like a dead bear for about twenty seconds, then leapt up and ran away top speed. The cancer apparently changed the dynamic for Dad. He never minded that sort of thing before. He usually celebrates the humpings, as if feeling a camaraderie with the twitchy strays. He seems to sympathize, watching them get dragged into our yard by female smells. He sometimes even waves good-bye like a cordial pimp, mistaking a dog's nervous glance backward as gratitude.

And he makes a point of allowing the younger shepherds to mount their mother at will, though it usually results in demented pups. Some are blind or lame or dead, and some are geniuses. I named one genius Timmy Thomas. He learned to sit, shake, and fetch when he was just a couple months old.

Mother goes out with a bucket whenever she sees inbreeding, to douse the dogs with freezing water. They break apart, howling, but the job is generally done by then.

The first time she did this, Dad asked, "What the hell did you do that for?"

"I don't want the kids seeing that."

"Seeing what?"

Mother lowered her voice, "Oh, for Christ's sake, they're screwing their mother out there!"

Dad laughed because she usually replaces the word *screw* with *squirrel*. He said, "I don't see Buffy minding."

"What's that supposed to mean?"

"I don't even know! But I'm sure it happens like this in the wild."

"This isn't the wild."

"Like hell!"

✻

A boy on a bicycle is staring from the far end of the parking lot. My sister's expression makes Dad think she's hurt herself. He's handing us pints of orange juice, but stops to ask if my sister cut her finger or something. She ducks behind the dumpster and hisses, "I know him."

What she means is that she loves him. She confesses this later to Mother. Then the boy ridicules her during recess. He calls her a "bum," so my sister sucker punches him in the throat.

The suspension is for three days. Then another week because she won't apologize. And she won't leave her room. Mother carries in her favorite meals on a big platter and talks to her.

Dad also talks, but takes a philosophical approach. He suggests she see shame as a concept, not just a feeling. It's a replacement emotion, like anger. We use it when we can't distinguish exactly how we feel. Hell, even people living on the street get embarrassed. A guy named Jim grins like a red-handed moron and jumps out of the dumpster at the first hint of confrontation. "When a box-boy sees him in the trash, Jim sees himself, and it's not a guy just looking for food. He sees a lowlife, because he's chosen an arbitrary social hierarchy over Self. Somebody, somewhere, made some random rules, and Jim feels guilty for breaking them! Even in such an extreme context. I mean, this poor guy sleeps on the sidewalk next to an industrial vent because it puffs warm air. But he still can't live by his own criteria. He still cares what people think!"

Mother asks Dad to try a little empathy. My sister only feels worse when he implies that her feelings aren't real. "Her heart's broken, for Christ's sake."

So Dad tries. He asks me to squat with him in a dumpster and picture the person we'd least like to see us. "I used to have this girlfriend who I really wanted to impress. . . ."

I say, "How about the president?"

Dad laughs, "I actually voted for that jackass. Last time I ever vote!"

"John Wayne?"

"Yeah, that's a good one. But it's not working. I guess I'm not programmed for shame."

Dad talks again with my sister. He tries to relate. If her heart hurts, that's all that matters. She should "go for it." Feel as ashamed as she wants. It holds significance for her, obviously. So the only way to figure it out is to "take it to the limit."

"I don't want any more trash, Dad."

✴

My sister tries to join Mother's strike. She starts referring to me in the plural: "Scabs." She learned this trick from Dad. When a mistake is made, Dad likes to call one person "ding-a-ling brothers."

But the hunger strike is over. Mother ended it without fanfare or any concession from Dad. When he saw her eating again, he offered her money to continue losing weight. Three dollars per pound for the first fifteen. Two dollars per for the second fifteen. And one dollar for every pound after that. Mother made nearly seventy-five dollars, then spent it on Dad.

I find this out in the ski lodge. Dad is talking to a German doctor who has tons of money, but very little love. The doctor's accent makes him sound smart. He's interested in Dad's Western recipe for happiness.

Dad tells him how clean American garbage is. He says things like, "This is a crack in society, and you can go live in that crack."

Then he says, "I paid my wife to lose weight, but she went and bought me gifts. This green sweater I really like. It's kind of neat that she could lose the weight, but it's no use giving her money if she just spends it on me. All she needed was the money motivation."

The German says, "Don't you think it's because she sees it's important to you?"

"No, I always try to act unconcerned about the fat. I never talk about it. It's always her trying to lose. Going on a million diets, which she's done all her life. Maybe I finally got concerned."

"Why now?"

"Because it makes her look fairly plump."

"You're concerned that the fat makes her look plump?"

Dad laughs. "Well, when you walk down the street with a plump woman, people wonder what you're doing, you know? I feel a bit awkward. I walk ahead of her."

"You're embarrassed."

"I would never admit that to her."

"Maybe you don't need to."

"Yeah, she probably knows. She's probably getting subliminal messages from me."

"Subliminal? Like walking ahead of her?"

"Right!" Dad laughs. "With my face all red!"

"I'm not sure that qualifies as subliminal, my friend."

"I guess not."

✱

Mother packs her bags over a note from Dad. He's angry about his birthday present. He gave Mother twenty dollars for her last birthday. She wanted to show him what it feels like to get twenty dollars, so she saved the bill and wrapped it up for his birthday.

Mother shows me Dad's note:

Thanks for giving me the finger for my birthday. Giving me back the same money I gave you. Not even a card! You bought yourself a tape player for my birthday. How quaint! In spite of your shit attitude week after week, I keep trying to be nice, but to no avail. God, you must hate me. I'm last on your list. There has always been a "we" for me. The money has always been "ours." You just don't want me to control it. Instead you want control. You want me to be like Ken or Warren. You want to be my Mother! But I'm not taking your shit anymore. Unless you can get your head

out of your ass and be a real person and give me some respect,
just stay away!

Mother gathers us at the front door to explain that her husband is a heartless bastard whom she can't stand for another second. She is moving to Oregon to be with her loving sisters. So we need to decide whom we want to live with. But first she'll find a motel room in town, so we have a little time to make up our minds. And she won't be upset if we choose Dad.

My brother and I beg. My brother says it'll be no fun without her. I describe all the things we'll start doing right. My sister says nothing, so Mother wants her opinion.

My sister shrugs. "I don't think you should leave."

My brother sobs with relief as Mother unpacks.

＊

She packs again in a couple days. She stands at the door for another exciting good-bye. This time we barely glance up from the television. From now on, she'll have to convince herself to stick around. And she does, after sitting in the car for an hour.

＊

The surviving pup has distemper. He shudders constantly and winds his eyes around like a little lunatic. Plus, every inch of his mouth is covered with white seed warts. Even his tongue. My sister convinces us that we can be infected with the warts from a single lick. So whenever the pup comes galloping up to play, my brother and I run for our lives.

When he dies, Dad says, "Don't worry, she'll have another batch soon enough."

Mother joins us for the funeral procession, which ends at the creek behind our house. Mother shuts her eyes to pray. Dad sets the pup in the water, and he floats away.

Look what you did.

I know, goddamn it.

Chapter 13

Bob drives up on a Suzuki 500. He doesn't know our address or phone number. He's in the parking lot of a restaurant called Anderson's Split Pea, preparing for his trip back. I say to Dad, "That looks like Bob." If I hadn't recognized him, he would've driven a total of fourteen hours for a bowl of split pea soup.

Dad shouts, "Bob!"

But that's wrong now. He's finally changed his name because of all the drunk-driving trouble. He won't say the new name in front of me. He says only, "I picked a Mexican one."

Bob has a little money, so the three of us go to a tavern. The waitress happens to be pretty, but she isn't happy about my age. She brings a pitcher of beer, but makes Bob "waste" a few of his dollars ordering a cheeseburger. There has to be food on the table if beer is being consumed in the presence of a minor.

Then they start drinking, and I learn several things.

Dad can't stand his marriage, but "intimacy" keeps him from leaving. "She gives herself fully to the situation, which makes her this sex queen, you know . . . unsurpassed in history."

Bob says, "Unsurpassed? What are you talking about?"

"It's unsurpassed."

"Do you have a feeling of intimacy outside of that?"

Dad thinks a moment. "If we want to feel close, that's the only thing she can enter completely into. Unconscious or whatever."

"Unconscious?"

"Unconsciously, I should say. But at the same time, she doesn't like me grabbing a part. A lot of times, that's my approach. I won't caress her on the cheek or anything. I'll grab a part, and that's what she hates. But that's what our relationship is. And it's extremely intimate."

"Why don't I believe you?"

"Probably because you never had it so good."

Bob laughs.

Dad says, "If you had it this good, you'd know it was the real deal!"

"Right. The kind of profound intimacy that starts with part-grabbing!"

"Well, I don't know how else to say it. It's this extremely intimate thing where both people are fully involved and everything disappears."

"Yeah, no kidding, man. It's sex! I've never had sex *without* feeling like that."

"Well, hooray for you! Then how come you don't know what I'm talking about?!"

"Because I've never had a serious relationship limited to that. I mean, Jesus Christ. You make it sound so unique. Everybody on earth feels like that during sex!"

"Well, hooray for everybody on earth."

✦

My response to Dad's birds and bees talk was "I ain't putting my wiener in no girl's Virginia."

This amused Dad, and he's been repeating it to people ever since. If the person is a man, they almost always say something like "Just wait!" or "We'll see about that!"

Now he tells Bob, who says, "Good luck!" and slaps his knees.

The waitress brings the cheeseburger and says, "This has to stay in front of him. House rules. If I look over and one of you is eating his . . ."

Dad convinces her to shut up by saying, "All right already!"

I got in trouble in kindergarten for passing on Dad's

description of sexual intercourse. The principal explained, "You'll have to keep that to yourself for now because kids your age aren't ready for that."

And I wasn't allowed to play with a neighbor friend in Huntington Beach for a couple months after breaking the news about Santa. The father was upset. Then Dad had to stop being friends with the father altogether when I passed on something Dad had said about God. The father's name was Stein Steinson. He was the palest person I've ever seen. His face skin seemed almost transparent. He drank during the day, and often rode his bicycle in circles in the middle of our street, singing. He once crashed the bike against our tree, then came up onto the porch and sat on the railing. He talked to Mother for a while before falling over backward. Five feet down into rose bushes. He came back up and sat in the same spot, then asked whether I wanted to sit on his lap.

I said, "No, thanks."

He asked again.

No.

When he asked a third time, Mother said, "Oh come on, don't you want to sit with Uncle Stein?"

I told myself, Maybe she's blind. Yeah. Maybe she can't see or hear.

Stein's son was named Teddy. Stein often asked Teddy to

hold pieces of lumber while he cut them with a circular saw. Wood chips would fly into Teddy's face, but he had stopped complaining because his father always made some comment about being a sissy.

When Dad and Stein stopped being friends, it was because Dad said that God wasn't all that nice.

This upset Stein because he had developed his own religion, and the most important tenet was that God was fair. Stein had convinced four people to join his church. Teddy told me that one of those people was his mother, so it was really only three. He slept at my house one night, after mentioning this to his father, who then slapped him in the face for being disrespectful.

＊

Bob remembers this:

They met Mother outside a bar called The Firehouse in Newport Beach, California. They had hot-wired a car in order to go drinking. When they saw two girls peeking into the doorway, Dad yelled, "Buy us a beer and we'll take you in!"

Mother's sister yelled, "You buy *us* a beer and we'll go in with *you*!"

So they checked their pockets and came up with two

dollars between them. They had stolen a car to party with two dollars.

"I get the small one," Dad said, meaning not Mother.

Dad explains to me, "Your mother was pretty big, and back then it wasn't so good to be with a tall woman. But Bob is even shorter than me, so he convinced me to give him the short one. We didn't want someone taller than us, and your mother was a towering inferno. She wasn't completely fat yet. She was medium, probably. Anyway, Bob got dibs."

Bob says, "Love at first sight."

"Yeah, I got stuck with her."

Mother wouldn't touch the one glass of beer Dad could afford. Mormons aren't allowed to drink alcohol or coffee. So Dad drained the glass and said, "Let's dance."

She wouldn't dance, either.

"But it was a joint!" Dad says. "Everybody was whipping up a storm, so I started dancing with this gal who was really swinging her butt around. I drank your mother's beer and danced with all the girls who were really going at it. I had a good time, but your mother was just sitting there. Eventually she wanted to go see my boat. I was diving for abalone back then and living on this boat. She thought that was neat, so I took her down."

Bob says, "Took her down?"

"No, I don't mean it that way. Sex was a long way down the road. I wasn't really interested."

✦

Mother brought her brother along for their first official date. Her brother is six foot eight. Dad put Mother in a wet suit, but couldn't get enough weights on her. "She kept trying to dive down. I put more and more weight on, but she wouldn't go down. She was too . . . um . . . buoyant."

She finally sank and stayed down for half an hour by herself, which is uncommon. It usually took about five minutes for first-timers to get spooked by all the sea life. Dad was impressed.

The brother asked if she was OK.

"I guess so," Dad said. "I still see bubbles coming up."

Afterward, when Mother tried to hand Dad the scuba mouthpiece, he said, "That's not mine. That's Richie's."

"And that upset your Mother because Richie was a black guy, and Mormons are fairly prejudiced. The funny thing is, when Richie came back, he was upset that a white woman had used his mouthpiece!"

Bob goes crazy, rocking back and forth. "Why'd you give her Richie's mouthpiece?"

Dad gives the same answer he'd given Mother at the time.

"I wasn't gonna give her mine!"

Bob continues going crazy.

＊

Dad brought a blanket for their second date. "I only had it so we could lay on the beach or whatever, but it got her worried. She always took a hatpin with her on dates. She kept it in her hair so she could jab guys if they got fresh. It was pretty hard to make any moves with this woman."

Bob says, "So you admit you wanted to make some moves?"

"Not especially. After that second date, she was upset because I was hanging back. First she was afraid of the blanket, and then she was mad because I wasn't pushing the issue. Apparently she thought it was time to make out. But I had other outlets."

"So why'd you keep seeing her?"

"I don't know. She was like a spare. I really didn't care, and she kept herself in abeyance because of that. Here was this spare on the side...."

"What do you mean spare?"

"A spare woman!"

"But the word spare implies ... I mean, you eventually *use* a spare tire."

"Yeah, if you have a blowout."

To accommodate Dad's eventual blowout, Mother traded in twenty-six years of virginity for instant pregnancy.

✳

As the waitress clears my plate, Dad tells her about my response to his birds and bees disclosure. She doesn't laugh. She looks at me and asks, "What's your name?"

"Dirk."

We wait to hear why she wants my name, but she just stares at me for a moment, barely nodding. Then she puts the bill on the table.

Dad says, "Not quite yet," about the bill, and orders another pitcher.

She says, "Then I'll have to leave this plate."

"That's fine."

Then the waitress gives me a quick smile from behind the bar, and for the first time, I consider the possibilities. A woman waiting for the rope tow yesterday was wearing a bikini top that looked like two spider webs. It was crocheted, and the knit wasn't tight, so a hard pink nipple poked out from the center of each web. The men in line were having mini–heart attacks over this. They couldn't stop whispering. One guy said, "She's doing it on purpose," which seemed to make it even better for him. It just seemed embarrassing to me, but now I found myself wishing that the waitress was wearing the same top. She seems to be thinking about me. She might be wondering about how I feel. So I try to imagine it. Maybe she wouldn't mind if I put my wiener in her Virginia.

Bob leans in to tell us about a book he read, in which a father sits down with his twelve-year-old son to say, "Your mother thinks it's time we had a little talk about the birds and bees. Remember what we did to those ladies in that ditch last Friday? Well, apparently the birds and bees do that too."

✳

In the morning, there's a good-bye note. Dad has gone back to Huntington with Bob. He needs a vacation from his vacation. Mother starts packing again, mumbling to herself.

Being forgotten, of all things, scares the living shit out of me. So I stand next to Mother. Just a little reminder that with one parent gone, it's customary for the other parent to look out for the kids. Mother notices me and stares. Then at my brother and sister. It works. She remembers us. "Pack your stuff. We're going to Oregon."

Dad takes vacations whenever things are going poorly with Mother, who calls them separations. One year it was

Cabo San Lucas to spearfish and lounge in a hammock. Next it was Hawaii, knowing Mother had always been dreamy for it. He toured "living reefs" on small borrowed catamarans. He bleached his hair white and got a perm, then wore a bandana so the hair would stick up like an old-fashioned haystack. Now it was back to our sunny hometown, leaving us to crawl under the A-frame every couple days with a small propane torch to unfreeze the water pipes. Mother always pretends she's going to do it until the last second, then hands me the torch. She doesn't fit under houses. The torch poofs when you light it. No matter how prepared I am for this, I always flinch.

Poof.

*

The night before we move, I find Mother trembling under her quilt. She perks up when I sit on the bed. She wants my opinion on something—a "silly" new habit of visiting a fantasy world every night. Her fantasy husband is named Larry. He has an OK job, and they own an OK house. She has the same children as in real life because "I would never trade you kids in."

Larry is not particularly good-looking, but he's respectful and attentive. He worries about money, and they plan together how to make ends meet. Whenever Mother brings home a few extra dollars from cake decorating, Larry buys her a little present because he feels guilty. He wishes she could just stay home and concentrate on the children.

Mother is thin. It's Larry who has the weight problem. His snoring took some getting used to, but now she can't sleep without it. The car needs some work, but it's reliable, and they almost have enough money saved for a second. Larry got offered a better job, but it meant moving to another city in the middle of a school year, so he turned it down. He knows how hard that sort of thing can be on children. Besides, Mother has made so many friends in the neighborhood. Nearly twice a month, they dine in with another couple, or Larry takes Mother to a restaurant. And when something is bothering either of them, they go to the other for advice or empathy. Larry is a good man, and they're happy to grow old together.

Mother asks, "Does that sound weird to you?"

"What?"

"Does all that sound weird?"

"I don't know. Not really."

She nods for a moment. "You're my golden boy."

"What?"

*

In the morning, we drive to a Greyhound bus station. Mother has decided to take only my sister and Buffy to Oregon. She tells us this as we load our suitcases into the belly of the bus. She wants to teach Dad a lesson by shipping down his two sons.

The bus is packed, so we can't sit together. The good-bye isn't as romantic as Mother would like because of an unpleasant moment with the bus driver, who asks about our ages. She needs to verify that we're old enough to travel alone. Mother answers, but is offended by the implication. "What are you saying?"

"I'm just doing my job."

"I thought your job was to drive the bus."

"I know what my job is, ma'am."

Mother hands us each a turkey sandwich and one dollar. "Good-bye, kids. I love you."

The first stop is a restaurant. Everyone shuffles in.

My brother and I sit on the curb to eat our sandwiches and breathe diesel exhaust. The bus is idling, but somehow we don't think to move. Earlier, we were too surprised to get upset, but now my brother cries a little.

My sandwich is wrapped in brown paper. It's just a lump of processed turkey between slices of white bread. No mayonnaise or mustard. No cheese.

I nudge my brother, "You wanna buy my sandwich?"

He laughs, but keeps his head down.

"I'll give you a dollar to eat mine."

He says, "It's the worst sandwich in the world."

"I know."

Chapter 14

Dad drives us straight to a market and climbs into the bin. We wait in the truck because the bus ride took nine hours and we couldn't sleep. Dad returns with two bashed cantaloupes and a box of candy bars covered with what looks like powdered detergent. There's something different about him. A new kind of abandon. It seems impossible that up to this point he's actually been reining himself in—holding back for the sake of the family. But here he is, grinning and offering us two clearly inedible items. As if to say, see what I mean? We can eat anything. Anything!

He goes back for more. There's an animal hospital next door. A veterinarian is kneeling behind an animal in the bed of a pickup. I can't tell what kind of animal it is, or what's being done to it.

My brother turns on the radio, then points to the veterinarian and says something.

"What?"

He repeats himself, but just as quietly. It's his favorite trick.

He categorically refuses to raise his voice. Muttering a sentence as many times as a person asks for it, then smiling at the irritation. It seems he's spoken only a handful of well-placed words during his entire life.

Ignoring Mother is another favorite. When she asks about a chore, he stares at cartoons like he's autistic. The louder Mother asks, the harder he stares. All she wants is a yes or no! Mother doesn't refuse to raise her voice. She sometimes suggests that he's just like his father. She sometimes gets upset enough to call him a "lazy shit," seeming on the verge of braining him against a wall. But my brother always takes it in stride, looking back and forth between the TV and Mother's frustration, as if he can't decide which cartoon is better.

I turn off the radio. "What?"

"I said that vet is doing some good butt work."

✳

A whistle comes from behind a concrete wall. Dad whistles back and waves good-bye to an employee holding a mop. The man shouts, "Que Lastima!"

Dad had asked the man to call him "There but for the grace of God go I," but he's Mexican and can't pronounce it. So Dad chose Que Lastima.

He waits to see if we know what it means.

"What a pity. It means what a pity. So he gets the joke."

He waits to see if we get the joke.

"See, I'm making fun of the embarrassment people have over me. They don't know what to do, but they feel this knee-jerk sympathy. A woman gave me a couple bucks the other day, and I took it, just like it was OK. And it was. She felt good. She wanted me to go buy a coffee and donut. And there's this woman who works at the Burger King there. She came out and asked what I was doing. I said getting something to eat. I had a sack of burgers. She said, 'Well, put that stuff back and come inside. I'll give you a burger and fries and a drink.' I thought that was nice, but then she offered to leave a broom by the back door. Every time I cleaned up the trash area a little, she would bring me a meal. But I didn't want a job. There's the stuff right there, you know? The food is right there. Why would I sweep up? Of course, she didn't know that defeats my purpose."

He opens one of the candy bars to show us that the detergent hasn't eaten through the wrapper. "See that? Perfectly good on the inside."

✳

We drive to my aunt's house. Two of Mother's eight Mormon sisters haven't moved to Oregon yet. Dad goes inside for a while, then slams the door on his way out.

With the next aunt, he stays inside longer. He doesn't bother slamming the door this time. And he doesn't start the truck right away. He just stares into space.

I say, "Where now?"

"Your mother called ahead and asked them to turn us away."

"What?"

"Can you believe that?"

"Where do you usually sleep?"

"On the beach. But I thought you kids would rather have a bed. Your mother wants me to learn about responsibility."

"Now what?"

"And both her goddamn sisters said it exactly the same way, like they rehearsed it."

"Now where?"

"What a stupid word. *Responsibility*."

✦

We bodysurf until the sun goes down, then try to sleep on a foam pad in the truck camper. Dad found the camper abandoned behind a high school. It doesn't fit his truck, so he "jimmy-rigged" it. My brother is allergic to almost everything, including abandoned camper dust. He flops around, making bubbling snot noises while Dad snores. So I bundle up in ski jackets I find packed behind the seat. I try to sleep on the sand next to the front tire, until police show up and explain through a loudspeaker on their car that vagrants aren't allowed on the beach after dusk. I roll under the truck to avoid being seen. But then the truck starts, so I jump up and climb inside.

Dad jams the gearshift. "Goddamn pigs."

✳

Next is Bob's house. There are two kegs of beer and so many devoted smokers that it appears the ceiling has caught fire. The smoke rolls. Bob invites us to sleep on his couches, but we'll have to wait until the party is over. Until then we should make ourselves completely at home.

Then Bob concentrates on two women who are stripping to loud music in his living room. One of them is on his coffee table. The other is at floor level with everyone else. Both the women are taking the crowd's advice. They're taking it all off.

A woman next to us comments on how cute two little boys look standing in the middle of so much debauchery.

I turn to ask Dad what debauchery is, but he's gone to visit the keg on the kitchen counter.

My brother sits in the corner and starts falling asleep. I try to enjoy the show, but the two women are not attractive. And one of them is super short, with a big forehead and thick hands. Then the music stops, and it's like some switch flips off inside the women. They are suddenly ashamed, grabbing for their clothes. Another song starts, but the switch won't turn back on. They wrap themselves up and hurry down the hallway. The crowd goes wild over their exposed buttocks running away.

"Now that's what I call naked!" Bob says. "Nobody's really naked until they don't wanna be." He follows the women, holding up a hand for his guests, as if to say, Don't worry, I'll take care of this huge problem.

✦

Dad's voice wakes me up. I'm in the corner next to my brother. There are only a few guests left. Dad is trying to make a bet. Apparently Bob had just taken the extra short stripper into his room and shown her a good time. Dad wants to bet Bob twenty bucks that the woman is retarded.

"No, she's just really drunk. Drunk people are always being mistaken for retards." Bob's laughter requires him to splash his beer.

Dad says, "But she might be a midget too. I think you just made love to a retarded midget."

Bob wags his head around, then sets his beer down in order to laugh properly. "Now that's funny! Made love . . ."

♦

Dad leaves us with his truck at the beach so he can make his morning rounds on a bicycle since it's such a nice day. Six hours later, with a bandaged head, he tells us this story:

"I was headed back with a rack of cottage cheese when somebody opened their car door. I had to swerve out into traffic, but there was this bus bearing down on me, so I swerved back and lost control. My head went right into the corner of a van. When I regained consciousness, there were all these cops and paramedics, so I told them 'No hospital.' The paramedic said there might be internal bleeding. I said I couldn't afford it. He said, 'Well, if you're a fast bleeder, it probably doesn't matter. You're already dead. But if you're a slow bleeder, you've got until morning. If I was you, I'd go.' So I acquiesced. They took X-rays of my head and wrote me down as Indigent. The doctor eventually said I was OK, so I took off down the street. I had to go get my bike from the cops. They'd taken it to their little cop shop. But this nurse came running out after me. I thought she was gonna hassle me about the bill, but she said, 'Sir, here's your cottage cheese!' She had about four cartons. So I said, 'Oh, no thanks, lady.' I had to walk about five miles. I didn't wanna carry that shit."

✴

We find a surfboard in a dumpster. There's no fin, and it's so waterlogged that I can barely lie on it and paddle, let alone catch a wave. The other surfers aren't missing fins. I know this because they keep flashing them in my face. They come right at me and turn at the last second, giving me really good looks at how sharp their fins are. They want to kill me for being a pale dork.

Then a big wave does me a favor. It snaps the leash running to my ankle and carries the board all the way to the sand, which allows me to give up. And I don't bother dragging the piece of crap back to where Dad and my brother are watching. I leave it bobbing in the froth.

Dad thinks it's funny. "What's the matter?"

I sit down. "It's pretty hard."

"So quit."

"I did."

But he can't stop chuckling.

"What's so funny?"

"I like the way you expected it to be easy."

"I didn't expect it to be easy! That stupid board doesn't work!"

"I know. Relax. That's what's funny. It's a hard sport to begin with. And then you've got this terrible board. . . ."

"Yeah. Ha ha!"

"Hey, don't get shitty about it."

"Look who's talking."

✳

We play Frisbee at our old playground, three blocks from our old house. Dad keeps an eye on a nearby family reunion. They are eating catered lasagna. Dad wants to tell me something, but waits until my brother wanders over to the swings.

When he first met Mother, she recognized him from a photo in the newspaper. He had jumped off a thirty-foot pier to save a boy face-down in the surf. Everyone else on the pier was just standing around saying, "My God!" So Dad jumped.

Mother was impressed and became impregnated. She wanted to get married, but Dad had just gotten divorced and had a bad taste in his mouth. So he made a deal. He would marry Mother on one condition. They must get divorced immediately following the wedding.

Mother wanted a baby more than anything. A legitimate baby. And Dad's deal would allow her to announce to her family, "We got married!" without it being a lie. So they drove to Tijuana and found an official who would marry and divorce them. Combined, the ceremonies took eleven minutes, and cost sixty-five dollars. Mother paid.

My sister was born. Two years later, me. Four years later, my brother came out blue, refusing to breathe until the doctor shook him violently.

Then one summer Bob was headed to Santa Barbara to marry his sweetheart. He invited Dad to come along and make it a double wedding. What the hell, Dad figured. They already had three kids anyway.

I interrupt. "Why are you telling me all this?"

Dad picks at a blade of grass. He watches my brother swing high enough to dangle and drop a little at each peak.

"Are you getting divorced?"

"Yeah, but everything's gonna be fine. It'll be better this way. She's going to Oregon."

"Is that why she sent us down here? Are we living with you now?"

"No. She doesn't know about the divorce yet. I just signed

the papers last week. I didn't want to wait, so I signed for her.
That way we can avoid a big fight about it."

"You forged her name?"

"No. I signed for her."

*

The family reunion breaks up at dusk, leaving a big tray of
half-eaten lasagna in the bin, under a pile of soda cans. My
brother turns two of the cans into loud shoes by stepping on
their centers. He walks around crunching and singing quietly,
"Jackpot, jackpot."

Dad washes used plastic spoons in the drinking fountain.
"I talked to this guy the other day who spends all day searching for cans. He was old and bent over. Eighty-something years
old. I told him I didn't understand. There was stuff to eat right
there. But he said, 'I gotta have the money.' He'd gotten some
donuts from the dumpster, but he fed them to the birds. He'd
rather find cans, then get money and buy the same donuts for
himself! I didn't understand that. I mean, he spent all day doing it. He lost his day. He could've gotten something to eat in
five minutes, then had the whole day! I don't know. Maybe he
didn't want the day. Maybe . . . I had a hard time with that."

Dad sets the picnic table. Napkins as plates. The spoons

are white.

"I guess he thinks that money has some kind of value. But all it does is get you things, and they're not even important things. I mean, money's OK. It can be an adventure, but how far can you go? You get a yacht, or whatever people do with a lot of money. Then what do you do? Are you happy?"

He rolls back tinfoil and serves the lasagna. It's still a little warm.

"There's a certain searching. Everybody's curious and looking. Everywhere you go, you see people looking. What are they looking for? I think it's right in front of them. Right there! The thing itself."

"What is it, Dad?"

He laughs. "Hell if I know!"

Part Three
La Grande, Oregon, 1977

Chapter 15

There's a welcoming party for my brother and me in La Grande, which looks like a national park. A valley of evergreens at the northeastern corner of Oregon. From the main highway, we saw only chimney smoke, then a population sign reading twelve thousand. Mother claims that seven thousand of them are Mormons. It's the first time I've seen Mother in blue jeans. She is smiling and almost not fat. Rededicating herself to the Church has given her the discipline to eat only cracked-wheat cereal for several months.

My aunts are waiting at my grandmother's house. They jump out to say Surprise, then line up for hugs. "Where's Bishop McKinley?" Mother calls out. "Tell him to make it seven thousand and four!"

There actually is a Bishop somewhere in the house. Mother is in a hurry to get us baptized because Dad has threatened to take his next vacation here, as soon as the ski season ends in Mammoth. Dad was "saved" as a teenager, and vowed to never let it happen to his children. Never.

My grandmother hushes everyone as the Bishop enters the living room. My grandmother is very old, but has beautiful hair. Not many people know this because she keeps it wound tight in a bun. In her room, the hair cascades past her waist, still a natural dark brown. I know this because I walked in on her while looking for a bathroom, then got scolded for not knocking. It was my second reprimand. The first was for hugging her legs when we arrived. I mistakenly thought she was in line for a hug, and knocked her off balance for a moment.

The most distinctive thing about my grandmother, though she has a friendly face, is that she has never touched me. I once mentioned this to Mother. She explained, "Honey, she has eighty-five grandchildren. It would take all day to hug every one of them."

✦

The Bishop has red hair. He positions my sister and brother on a sofa, but makes the mistake of trying to guide my sister by the shoulder. She rears back as if to punch him in the face, then decides not to.

Mother and I are gestured onto a velvet love seat beside the sofa. Everyone else backs against the nearest wall and sort of tilts their eyes down until the room feels like an elevator.

The Bishop sits on a dining chair in the center of the floor. He welcomes us and says that Mother is very excited about her children joining the church because she wants to reserve our seats in the Celestial Kingdom, which is the highest level of heaven. Without us being baptized, that wouldn't be possible. We would be relegated to the lowest level. And from the highest level, where God Himself resides, Mother would have to settle for only occasionally hearing our voices in the distance, for eternity.

Baptism is a wonderful thing, but it's important that we understand how it will start a tab with God. Nothing has been a sin yet because we haven't officially started distinguishing between good and evil. Once we join, everything will go on our spiritual record. And to erase misdeeds, we will have to repent. But, unlike the Catholics, we have to mean it. The Mormon God knows when you're just going through the motions. And once you're in, that's it. You can be excommunicated for horrible mistakes, but that only means you can't attend services. You will still be listed among the fellowship. You cannot quit the Church. He asks, "Do you have any questions so far?"

My sister has one. "Why don't people just get baptized on their deathbeds, to avoid the whole hassle?"

This gets a big laugh.

The Bishop smiles, "It doesn't work that way."

He assigns us to the Third Ward on a probationary basis, then asks for the bearing of testimony. Several aunts describe what a huge blessing Mormonism is. When Mother tries, she starts like the others—"I would like to bear my testimony that I know this church is true, that Joseph Smith is the true prophet. . . ."—but is overcome by emotion when she gets to the part about finally being with her sisters again. Her family.

"Goddamn," Dad likes to say, "how come whenever your mother says *family*, she never means us?"

✶

Our rental is on a dead-end street near the Grande Rhonde River. It's actually a trailer home subsidized by the Church. I realize this when it's time to unfreeze the water pipes with the propane torch. Poof. I've been on enough jobs with Dad to know what a foundation is supposed to look like. Ours is only occasional stacked cinder blocks, hidden by a skirt of plywood siding. A few bored teenagers could push our house over.

When I tell Mother this, she says, "Well, that's OK, right?"

"Sure."

"Beggars can't be choosers."

"I'm just telling you."

"We're lucky to have a place at all."

"OK."

✳

Aunt Carol arranges for me to accompany my cousin's Boy Scout troop on an informal trip to the Tri-Mountain Athletic Club, where I can get to know other Mormon boys. The troop is organized and supported by the Church. The scoutmaster is a grown man named Gary, who leads us straight to a Jacuzzi. All the scouts keep their shorts on, but Gary decides it's best to remove his. That way he can secretly press his rear hole against one of the underwater jets.

My cousin and I are using our hands as water squirters to sting each other's eyes when Gary offers to show us a trick. He climbs out of the Jacuzzi and says, "But don't tell anybody . . ." He gets on all fours and returns the water, in an arc, back into the Jacuzzi.

We consider this hilarious. Nobody makes the connection that Gary's rear is where he stores his dung, and that we are now relaxing in human dung. We simply give credit where credit is due:

"Gary can pee out his butt!"

＊

My sister discovers a new use for those hollow, tipless arrow shafts. She wants to know how far a shaft can enter a nose hole before it tickles brain. She promises to be gentle, swearing—her hand on the Book of Mormon on the television—to drown me in the river if I don't sit still. She eases the shaft in, then gives it a nice jab, filling the end of it with nasal meat.

With Mother stuffing and restuffing toilet paper in my nose, it takes twenty minutes for the bleeding to stop. There is no question in Mother's mind that it was completely unintentional.

I plead the contrary. I try to explain my sister's new strategy of continual accidents.

Mother says, "Oh, honey, don't be silly."

So I sit in the closet awhile, and eventually come up with a theory. Mother feels so hurt and disregarded by her husband, there is a sprinkle of revenge in seeing any male, even her son, with blood spurting from his face.

But then I notice a pile of postcards on the floor. My theory is wrong. The top card is just a week old. It's from Dad, and says this:

Hon,

Your communications are very welcome so don't worry about babbling on. I can't wait to get there, but won't come until I can get some money. I need a good welcome. I have missed a few days writing so I guess your letters stimulate me (to write). Sure happy about the new slender you. Can't wait for some of that "good stuff."

All my love

P.S. Your envelope decorations are great.

✱

Six days before Dad's arrival, his children are dunked in a baptismal font adjacent to the men's restroom of the Church of Jesus Christ of Latter-day Saints.

Chapter 16

Dad breezes into town on a Sunday with a full head of hair. We're leaving for church, and Mother won't let us out of the car because we're late. Her lipstick is blood red. "He thinks he can just waltz in." She's having trouble with the stick shift. The car lurches a few times.

Dad's truck bed is packed high with boxes, which are roped excessively. Bob once asked Dad to tie off his truck during a move. Since Dad had spent time on boats, Bob figured he was good with knots. Less than a mile into the drive, Bob watched in his sideview mirror as half his household belongings spread out over the highway. He didn't stop to retrieve anything because several large items struck other cars, and then several cars struck each other. Bob sped up and took the next exit, then called Dad from a tavern.

Dad responded, "Hey, man, I did you favor! Most of that stuff was pretty shitty."

Dad does a little hello dance for us, hands in the air, until he realizes that Mother isn't going to stop. He shouts as we roll

past, "Hey, wait! I have a good surprise!" He looks deflated a
moment, then resumes the dance through the rear window.

"Did you hear that?" my brother says. "He has a surprise."

"Yeah, he's full of surprises, honey."

✳

Scoutmaster Gary is also my Sunday school teacher. This
week's lesson is on tithing, but first he wants to dismiss recent accusations in the national press that the Church is racist.
Mormon congregations are divided according to geography.
This allows people with nice homes to worship with other
people with nice homes. We were placed in the Third Ward
because of the shitbox we live in, and because of all the shit-
boxes around it.

Gary says there have been recent suggestions in the press
that Ward boundaries are drawn for racial reasons, so that
white people can worship with other white people. He wants
us to know that this is a hurtful lie.

There is one black woman in our Ward. She has nine children. She seems very proud, but sits every Sunday alone in a
church full of white people. Gary says it's because of tithing.
Mormons give ten percent of their income to the church. This
enriches the church, and the rules are that food will be given

to those who are not enriched. The black woman's husband is dead. "She became a Mormon," Gary says, "so that her children can have something to eat."

But she never brings her children to church, which is smart. They would hear, during playtime in the gym, things like this:

"Hey, Jerry, where'd you get that hat?"

"Stole it off a dead nigger."

Or:

"Louie Moon is an anus baby."

Louie hears this a lot at school. Louie is one of the woman's children. At first I thought they were simply calling him stupid—*shit for brains* and that sort of thing. But they are claiming that his skin, because of the abnormal location of his gestation, had been stained.

Gary explains that Church doctrine is not designed to segregate colored people. Colored men are not allowed to hold the priesthood simply because they are descendants of Cain, who killed his brother Abel for no good reason. God wanted Cain's lineage to always remember this sin, so God marked them. He turned them brown.

✳

Dad's surprise is a rented white farmhouse on twenty acres, along with a promise to stay clean. No more trash. We will farm instead. "Hey, free food is free food, right? I lived off the land in Mexico by spearing fish, and in the city by dumpster diving. Now it's the country."

There's a huge red barn and a horse corral, a creek splitting the property in half, a chicken coop, a rusting yellow tractor, and a shed filled with large sharp metal things the tractor can drag. Wild asparagus grows along a side fence. Raspberry bushes and rhubarb border the creek. There's a line of weeping willows sixty feet tall.

Dad says, "The first thing is to get some animals. Goat's milk is really good for you. In fact, I saw an article on how to make cheese. And look at these trees!" There's a five-acre grove of peach, apricot, cherry, pear, and apple trees. "We'll be up to our eyeballs in fruit. We'll just plant a few crops, gather some eggs. Whatever it takes, right?"

Mother finally speaks. "Isn't farming just about the hardest job in the world?"

"Oh, Christ. Don't say job."

Chickens come first. My sister likes to feed them leftover fried chicken. She tosses them little pieces and says, "Cannibals," which gives me an idea. I put myself in charge of grating cheese for taco Tuesday. I grate skin from calluses on my thumbs, then sprinkle it over my sister's tacos. While she eats, I say to myself, "Cannibal." When she asks what the hell I'm grinning about, I keep quiet. Otherwise she would avenge my revenge. It's not all that satisfying, but it allows me the distraction of thinking, whenever she's stepping on my neck, "This is nothing. You've eaten human thumbs."

Next are goats. Then a horse, which Dad says is mine so he can pencil the fifty dollars into his book of poetry. There's a section in back where he keeps track of money his children owe him. He credits us three dollars for every hour we spend working the farm, but keeps us in the red by debiting school supplies and shoes. When my sister saw him opening the book to write down ice cream cones for us, she dropped hers into a trash can.

"Why'd you do that?"

"You can't debit me. I didn't eat it."

"Jesus." Dad got the cone out, wiped off debris with my brother's napkin, and ate it himself.

My horse is a Welsh pony named Honeycorn. She's terribly uncooperative. If I ride near the clothesline or a low branch, she charges and tries to take my head off. Near the creek, she stops abruptly to throw me in. She puffs out her belly whenever I cinch the saddle. This way, when she exhales, the saddle swings under and drops me to the ground, where she can trample me. She's like a circus horse, but all her tricks are evil. Dad charged me fifty dollars for my sister in horse form.

So I borrow another fifty to have her mounted by an Arabian stallion, whom Honeycorn immediately kicks in the testicles. This upsets the stallion's owner because he makes his living selling the contents of those testicles. The penis is a gigantic floppy thermos laced with purple veins. After a lot of maneuvering, and a few mind-boggling power thrusts, Dad feels we have been given our money's worth. Honeycorn seems unhappy, but I am looking forward to a nice baby horse that doesn't want to kill me.

✦

I tell my cousin about the spectacular horse humping, and he tells Scoutmaster Gary, which prompts our next Sunday lesson on "fornication." This is one of the things young boys should try to avoid. Fornication corrupts the soul. We would be better off abstaining until after marriage, when it is no longer spiritually dangerous.

We have no idea what fornication means.

Gary says that even after marriage, certain things are considered sinful. Variations that shouldn't be performed even with one's wife. When we are older, we will learn about the guidelines, which will help us reach the Kingdom of God. Gary describes the three levels of Heaven, the lowest of which is supervised by the Holy Ghost. If we choose to fornicate, that is the highest level we can hope to reach, and only through exhaustive repentance. The middle level is run by the Son of God, Jesus. If we only occasionally touch ourselves, though it's profane, we still might make it into this second level. A few of the boys giggle, which irritates Gary. "To live forever with God Himself, you have to be pure! You have to honor the temple God has given you. Your body!"

Someone finally speaks up. "What's fornicate?"

Gary ignores the question, thinking we know full well what it is. He goes on to the worst type of fornication, the type encouraged most by the devil, who wants all boys to join him in roasting hot Hell. On the totem pole of sin, this one is right near the top, second only to murder and renouncing one's faith. "Homosexual fornication."

Finally, because of our blank stares, he asks for a show of hands. How many of us don't know what fornication is? Everyone raises a hand, which only irritates him more. He seems to think it's a conspiracy. He thinks we're making fun of him, so he stomps to the chalkboard and writes this:

FUCKING.

"There. Are you happy now?"

＊

Dad's lack of anger over our baptisms is a little eerie. He seems only baffled, sitting in his lawn chair each Sunday to start waiting before we've even left. Then he jumps up to welcome us back, acting stunned that anyone could return safely from church.

But this time his chair is empty. There's a cardboard sign nailed to the big apple tree. Buffy comes out from under the house, whining with excitement. I indulge my new habit of watching for signs of her cancer. A limp, lazy eyes, blood on her tail.

The cardboard sign reads *Dad's Church.*

My sister asks, "What does that mean?"

Mother says, "I don't want to know."

Chapter 17

The first meeting of Dad's Church is also the last. It consists of a visit to a funeral parlor to see a Mormon missionary who flipped forward on his ten-speed and broke his head open.

I overheard most of the argument through the master bedroom door. Dad said religion might have been bearable when we were younger, but now we needed to start using our minds. So for every hour we spend in church, we would spend an hour with him, learning a scientific view of the universe. He's entitled to his share of influence. Mother said "No!" and cried a little, then agreed when Dad threatened to ban church altogether.

The funeral director shakes Dad's hand. "Such a shame."

"Yes," Dad said.

"I'll leave you alone to say good-bye."

"Yes. Thank you."

This funeral director performs with an oldies rock group each weekend at a bar called My Wife's Place. He shares lead vocals with his identical twin. The band is called the

Coffee Brothers.

Dad gestures to the open coffin and introduces us. "Kids. Death."

"He's in heaven?" my brother asks.

"No. Touch him."

My brother doesn't feel like it.

But my sister does. She puts her fingertip against the swollen cheek, then looks at her finger. "Gross."

"Exactly," Dad says.

✸

The hour isn't up, so Dad sits us under our apple tree to describe the incomprehensible size of the universe and the relative insignificance of earthlings. "Some of the stars in the sky don't even exist anymore because it took millions of years for the light to reach us."

My brother says, "Jimmy from school said rain is God's pee."

"There is no God, sweetie. Jim is lying. There's a God in the Bible, but he's just a made-up character, and a mean one at that. He made people a certain way, then banished them from paradise for simply being themselves. That's not a God. That's a poor baby."

Mother is on the front porch, biting her lip.

"And later he drowned almost the entire planet for the same reason. I'd make a better God than that. Any of us would."

❋

Mother arranges an emergency meeting with the red-haired Bishop. In his office, she explains the "situation." She isn't sure which is worse—not coming to church, or "letting a husband frighten my sweet babies with Atheism."

There's a photograph of Jesus on the wall. A crowd is kneeling around him, and he looks bored out of his mind.

The Bishop tells Mother, "Remember, family always comes first."

One of the Bishop's responsibilities is to interview all the young boys every six months, to find out how their young lives are progressing. The important question—the one I've been warned of—is "Have you found yourself yet?"

According to the Bishop's flat-faced son, it actually means this:

"Have you started playing with your pecker?"

Playing with your pecker is a sin, so the Bishop's son advised me to respond, "What do you mean?" Then the Bishop will change the subject because he doesn't want to put any ideas into any heads.

It worked. The Bishop said, "Never mind."

The Bishop's son also told me about his older sister, who came home at midnight one night with a torn dress. She is fourteen. She went on a date without permission. Mormons cannot date until they're sixteen. The tear in her dress did not make her Bishop father think, *Something bad must've happened to her.* It made him think, *She put herself in a position to allow bad things to happen.*

He immediately drove his entire family to the hospital so that a doctor could take a look at his daughter's private area. He wanted proof of the virtue she claimed was still intact.

The doctor was an old friend of the Bishop's. They had dug irrigation ditches together in college. After the examination, the doctor patted the Bishop's shoulder and whispered the bad news. His daughter's privates had gone public.

When the girl winced out into the hallway in her ruined dress, the Bishop turned and walked out to the car, where his wife was waiting in a bathrobe with the younger children. The girl had been raped. It will be almost ten years before anyone knows this, because it will be almost ten years before anyone asks.

Her brother tried to cheer her up. "Maybe Dad won't punish you."

＊

The Bishop chooses me, the oldest male, to represent the children. He asks, "How do you like your father's church?"

"It's OK."

But I notice Mother's gaze and realize the impact of my answer. Having the children on her side is crucial. The secret torture question of the house has become "Who do you like better, Mom or Dad?" When my brother is asked this repeatedly, he sobs. So I add, "But real church is better."

That seals it. Mother's mind is made up.

And the Bishop agrees. "I'd rather you take a break from services than split up a family. Besides, there are plenty of fellowship events the children can enjoy without it being considered Church. If you know what I mean."

Mother thinks a moment.

"You know what I mean?"

"I think maybe I do, Bishop."

＊

Fellowship events are things like scout meetings and campouts. Mother/daughter picnics. Softball games. There is a weekly dance in the church gymnasium, where we hear "MacArthur Park" by Donna Summer and "Everybody Was Kung-Fu Fighting." Chaperones prowl the dance floor during slow songs, enforcing the "six-inch rule" by prying kids apart. Pleats are popular with the boys because they help disguise the hydraulics in our pants.

We all want to dance with a girl named Tina because she is very kind. She uses the heel of her hand to knead aching erections during slow songs. She feels sorry for us, and that makes her beautiful. She wants to end the suffering. We are miniature bottles of champagne, and she wants to pop every cork. If she can't succeed before the chaperone breaks it up, her dance partner often hurries to the toilet next to the baptismal font to finish the job himself. There is ridicule waiting when he comes out, even from boys who did the exact same thing five minutes earlier.

I can't work up the courage to dance with her. I dance only with my sister. We spell out Y-M-C-A with our arms. The chaperones think the Village People are simply exuberant performers. If they knew the truth, the record would get snapped in two. Olivia Newton-John's hit *Let's Get Physical* has already been banned.

Then Tina gets banned. I'm in the corner, pretending to be on the verge of dancing with her, when two of the chaperones escort her outside. Her friends decided to rat her out. They're tired of never being asked to dance.

✦

When I get home from the dance, Dad waves me frantically into the barn. Our baby goat has broken off one horn. Dad pins her down and tells me to hold her there. No matter what. Don't let go. Blood is gurgling from the horn stump like a weak drinking fountain. Dad runs an extension cord from the far wall. Rather than call one of those crooked vets, he plugs in a soldering iron. He uses the word *cauterize*, and kneels down to burn the stump closed. The goat bucks like crazy. It's the worst thing I've ever smelled. And it's the worst sound I've ever heard. A very human groan that turns into a garbled blare, then gradually back to a groan as she gets sleepy and dies.

"Shit," Dad says. "OK, you can let go now."

Chapter 18

Dad can't convene his church without the opposing Sunday school, so he keeps us in the loop by slipping poems and letters to God under our pillows:

Dearest Lord,

May I remind you that I got Saved at Forest Home many years ago, and in spite of subsequent years in which I spoke of you in less than flattering terms, I will, on my deathbed, probably be the biggest kiss-ass son of a bitch you have ever encountered. Not that you have an ass (the term is figurative); but the way we are getting shit on down here, I figure it has to be coming from somewhere. A little reassurance on your part would assuage the insecurities of my agent, Jesus, about his cut in the action. He's worried about your image. We see a lot of "God is good" plaques down here. We don't see "God is nice" or "God is smart." Why not? Maybe those pesky Bible verses that show you killing people, or worse, in a pique of rage, gave everybody the wrong impression. People won't do what I want either, so I can sympathize. But listen, *you're getting a lot of bad press. So get a hold of a big bottle of white-out and obliterate said verses. While you're at it, white-out the whole thing, and yourself too. Oops. Gotta go.*

After finding this letter, Mother ups the ante with a trip to the center of the universe—Salt Lake City, Utah.

"The Mormon Las Vegas," Dad says.

Every six months, the Bishop ships a busload of children to the Salt Lake Temple, where they engage in a mass baptism for the dead.

Mother walks me onto the bus and sits me next to Scoutmaster Gary, who will serve as our spiritual advisor. The purpose of the trip, Gary explains to my cousin and me, is to give people who died without accepting God a second chance. These poor souls are given a final shot in Purgatory, which is like an intermediary wasteland between Heaven and Hell. If a still-living person is baptized on their behalf, and the dead soul accepts, they can squeeze into the lowest level of heaven.

My cousin says, "They're just waiting in Purgatory?"

"It's sad," Gary says. "Millions of them."

I ask, "How could a dead person not accept? They're just sitting there in Purgatory, right?"

"You'd be surprised."

✦

At the first rest stop, Gary uses a pay phone, then tells us about a Salt Lake boy who had been attacked by a card table a few hours earlier. The table supported a Ouija board, which the boy was using to locate information about his future. The information was supplied by Satan and funneled through the Ouija board. The story was relayed to Gary by the local Salt Lake Bishop, who had stepped in to save the boy. The Bishop asked Gary to warn all the incoming youngsters that Satan was in the area.

Gary reminds us that the only protection against Satan is this command: "In the name of the Father and the Son and the Holy Ghost, I demand that you be gone!"

This is what the Salt Lake Bishop used to stop the attack. The boy had gone too far, so the card table rose up and beat him within an inch of his life. But then the Bishop said the magic words and the table clattered to the floor.

My cousin asks, "Is the boy OK?"

"He's in the hospital. It's touch and go."

I ask, "What's *too far*?"

"What?"

"You said the boy went too far."

"Oh, yeah. I was afraid to ask."

✳

The baptizing is performed in male/female shifts so that our skin doesn't become pruned. Each child is dunked for approximately twenty-five dead people, then sent to a bench to dry off and wait for the next session. There are separate male and female benches, but the font is coed. During the female shifts, we all fold our hands over our laps and pretend to be cold. But really we are hiding quivering erections.

My cousin keeps whispering, "T.H.O." This is a secret code. It stands for Titty Hard-on. The girls' baptism outfits are like nightgowns, and underwear is disallowed. When the gowns get wet, they become transparent. So what the Bishops think is a mass saving of lost souls is actually one of the longest wet T-shirt contests in recorded history.

✳

We sleep in dormitory bunks in a gymnasium. Gary stops by to say that when he was in Vietnam, the first lesson he learned was to shave every single day. Otherwise, he mistook the sound of scruff against his collar for the sound of ambushing Gooks.

Then he whispers, "Remember those variations I told you about? We were talking about fornication, and I said there were certain things you shouldn't do even after marriage. Remember that?"

My cousin says, "Yeah."

Gary asks me, "You remember?"

"Yeah."

"You wanna know what one of them is?"

We look at each other and shrug.

"Well, sometimes my wife . . . let's see, how do I put this? Instead of wanting my thing in the normal place, she'll ask me to put it in her mouth for a while. She repents about it in the morning, and I'm only telling you because it's one of those things that everybody struggles with. Following the straight path is never easy, especially when your wife keeps asking you. And the amount of repentance depends on how far she goes. Sometimes it's not just for a while. She'll keep going, and then swallow the result. You know what I mean, right? You know about that?

"Anyway, I thought you should know because I just caught two of your fellow scouts doing to each other what my wife sometimes does to me. What do you boys think about that?"

We say nothing.

"Well, don't pass this around because most of the other kids aren't as mature as you guys."

We wait for him to leave before we start giggling.

*

I return home to the news that Buffy has been suffering mild attacks. Dad seems eager to tell me this. He asks, "How was Utah?"

"Fine."

"Great, because Buffy keeps getting stiff and falling over. She wiggles around for a while, but then gets up and seems fine." He waits for me to say something. "Looks like her problem is spreading." He waits some more. "I guess she's not getting better, huh?"

It takes me a moment to figure out what he's getting at.

Looks like your God has decided not to save your dog.

Chapter 19

Mother was right about farming being horribly difficult. Dad makes up his mind to quit after a near-accident with a baling machine, which we're pulling behind the tractor through our alfalfa field. The twine mechanism keeps malfunctioning. Each bale of hay explodes as it exits. When Dad reaches in above the conveyor belt, his sleeve momentarily snags. It looks for a moment like he will be dragged headfirst into the machine. Then he's suddenly free. He turns to me with his shirtsleeve torn off at the shoulder. "Wow. Fuck this."

I'm riding my colt when Dad says he's thinking about going back to construction, but as a contractor this time instead of a carpenter.

I named the colt Saber. He's as gentle and playful as a puppy. I can ride bareback without a bridle. He just goes where he wants, and I lie back in the sunshine.

Mother gave two requirements for taking Dad back. No more trash, and she wants to own a home. Dad knows a guy who's trying to unload some land, and the market is depressed.

In California, the requirements for becoming a contractor were exhaustive. In Oregon, it's about as difficult as obtaining a driver's license.

"But the real point is, everybody's so afraid to quit. They even turned *quit* into a bad word. That's how people spend their whole lives doing a job they hate. They think if they quit, it's the same as failing. But the only way to try something new is to stop what you're doing, right?" He scratches behind Saber's ear. "Remember that. I don't want you to ever be afraid of quitting."

*

He buys a blue van from a failed Mormon carpenter. The van is painted with various construction scenes. Dad changes only the business name. He paints *Economy Builders* in green. One of the scenes shows the failed Mormon holding up a sign that introduces him to everyone he drives past. The sign says, "Hi, I'm Dick." Dad doesn't change this.

I'm with Mother and two aunts when Dad drives past, honking. He seems proud of his new self-employment.

One of the aunts notices the *Hi, I'm Dick* sign. She says, "You sure are," and they all laugh.

✦

Mother invites my sister into the master bedroom for a lesson about respecting one's elders, then makes an odd decision. She tries to spank my sister, whose insolence has become unbearable. She has taken to blurting "Suck shit!" every time she sees Mother. No matter what. "Suck shit." But the spanking goes poorly.

I stay close to Mother that evening, waiting for her to say something, so I can say, "Maybe we should talk to Dad about it." But she keeps quiet. I am pretending that she fought with my sister to protect me. Mother is pretending that nothing happened.

Then she tries again the next day. After the first "suck shit," she corners my sister in her room. I listen through the door. There are no slapping sounds or hair-pulling squeals this time. Just grunting and the thump of fists.

My sister emerges with blood in the corner of her mouth and a red blotch below one eye. But she seems pleased.

Mother has no marks, but looks dumbstruck.

My sister later whispers a description of the fight. She punched Mom strictly "in the tits."

By continuing to pretend nothing happened, Mother officially drops rank in the family hierarchy. My sister is now second-in-command, and she verifies this in the morning. When I take the last of the milk, she lifts my glass and pours it over my plate of pancakes, then waits. She waits for Mother to say something. Mother just hands me a kitchen rag and returns to the griddle, confirming that from then on, whenever I go to Mother with blatant injustices, she will say, "Just try to stay away from her, honey. We all know she doesn't play fair."

✦

Mother took her beating as a sign. She begins preparing for the Second Coming. At first, she simply wants to be the one driving us to school. "Make it a great day!" She wants to cook the gooners. She wants to tuck us in with stories about Jesus, who always makes a big impression with his calm demeanor and the wise sayings he's able to think up on the spot.

Then Mother asks for help in the kitchen, assembling emergency kits with our names on them. Flashlights, granola, first-aid pouches, combs, purified water, licorice. She wants help canning peaches and pears that drop in the grove. We dry cherries and apricots on cleaned screens taken from windows. We smash apples into cinnamon applesauce. We prepare cracked wheat for breakfast as practice. Mom wants us to be prepared for the scenario that will make eating cracked wheat necessary, which Dad had described as something like this:

God will say "Enough already!" and open up Hell, temporarily releasing the devil and his crew to pillage the Earth and devour the sinners. Afterward, Jesus H. Christ will stroll along and holler into the cellars of all the Righteous who were smart enough to take cover. He will announce that the coast is clear. He will congratulate them on having just inherited the Earth, which is being renovated back into a paradise, as originally planned. They will be saved not just because of their righteousness, but because they had plenty of supplies. You can be Mother Teresa, but unless you have enough cornbread mix to outlast Satan and his bloody monkeys, you'll get chewed up and swept away with all the other scum.

✴

By lying to the widow of a Mormon businessman who died in the Eastern Oregon State swimming pool, Dad acquires her land for "pennies on the dollar." Dad was in the swimming pool, unsuccessfully negotiating a lower price for the land, when the man suffered a stroke. Dad pulled him from the pool and administered unsuccessful resuscitation.

At home, Mother thinks he's distraught because his face is bright red, so she tries to console him.

Dad says, "What the hell are you talking about?"

After the drowning, Dad had dried off with a new towel, purchased at Sprouse-Ritz for twenty-five cents. The towel transferred the bulk of its red dye to Dad's skin. So he hurries over to console the widow, hoping she will also mistake his stained face for grief. He brings along a document outlining the proposed land deal refused by the dead Mormon. "He was about to sign it," Dad tells the widow, "when he was taken."

The widow signs, and Dad is able to get a construction loan, though his credit is horrendous, because of the ridiculously low price. Even if Dad defaults the next day, the bank will make a terrific profit.

Dad plans to draw a salary from the loan while building a large, inexpensive home. We will live in it during construction to avoid paying "double rent." Dad tells Mother she can design the layout of the rooms, and we can all pitch in. She loves the idea of a family building their own house.

Dad pulls me aside to make a suggestion. It's probably better if we don't tell Mother that the house will be sold the instant it's finished.

Chapter 20

Mother delivers her version of the birds and bees in the form of a typewritten letter, prompted by a night I spent in her bed because my sister was feeling extra torturous. Dad was sleeping in the barn, angry about the purchase of a flowery pre-owned sofa. My first wave of persistent erections had swept in like a flock of bats, planting a sudden inexplicable interest in Mother's nightgown.

My stomach churned as I alternated my knees up next to her leg. She would think I was running in a dream. I would catch the nightgown with a knee and drag it up a little. I wasn't sure why I wanted this, but it went on for quite some time, without success.

"Honey?"

I stopped running and held my breath.

"Are you trying to lift my gown?"

I turned my back to her.

"What's the matter?"

I hit the bed. "I wasn't doing anything."

"OK."

"I was exercising my legs!"

"OK. Night, night."

✸

She leaves the letter on my pillow the next day. It says this:

Dear Dirk,

As an adult I have more experience and therefore I know where some of life's pitfalls are. One of these areas is the sexual area. As a young man you think you know what there is to know, but you have no idea how strong the sex drives are, and I have a parent's responsibility to make you aware and strong enough to be able to control your life and not have your life control you.

The world's word for intercourse, Dirk, is F------. That is not my word. My word is Making Love. The wild loose boys prefer to call it the other word. Why do you suppose that is?

You can experiment with sex, and if you're lucky and things go well, it feels very good. You can do that with lots of girls and lots of times you'll feel good. Or you can use sex only when you want to show a very special person how you feel. That's when it's making love. Making love is a way to show someone you love him so much you want to be part of him. There are lots of ways to show someone you LIKE them. You talk and share private jokes, you smile at each other from across the room, you hold hands. But making love is more than all those things. It's the only way you can be as close to another person with your body as you can be with your mind. That's when you know you're in love, when you want that kind of closeness.

Dirk, what I want for you is the best of everything. V.D., abortions, unwanted marriages are facts of life, but if you choose wisely, they will never be facts of your life. You will never know the shame or heartbreak these things bring.

Whatever others do, don't let them shame you into trying to keep up with them. Don't turn lovemaking into F------. Don't make it as ordinary as a handshake. Intercourse isn't an afternoon or evening sport, or a way of scratching an itch. Intercourse is a language. It's using your body to say I love you. Wait for that.

You have seen your father and me go through some rough times. I truly believe it is the knowledge of complete faithfulness to each other that has allowed us to weather the storm.

I also feel a need at this time to warn you of something you may or may not have experienced already. That is the girl who is not a wholesome girl. You may have already experienced the type of girl who tries to tempt you or get you excited either in the way she acts or the way she dresses. The best advice I can give you about this type of girl, Dirk, is to run like hell.

Son, I am not pushing you into girls, or greatly worried about your involvement with them. I just know the pressures that are brought the youth of today. These things I have tested, and they have brought only happiness. I know if you use them, they will work as well for you.

Please don't feel that I don't want to talk to you about this, because I do. I want you to always feel free to ask me questions and relieve your doubts. Remember, I was a girl once, and if you have any questions I am here for you.

Much love,

Mom

*

I stand on my bed to take stock. It looks bigger in the mirror, framed by a bony torso. My brain swirls with a kind of invincibility. I cock it down with my thumb and let it spring back, enjoying the possibility that Mother could walk in at any second. I'm a robust criminal, and Mother might be accompanied by pretty ladies from church. A Mormon Tupperware party. Mother will be proud and terrified of my fierce organ. The ladies will mistake me for a dangerous male model. They will gasp and inadvertently unseal their Tupperware.

But then Mother does walk in.

I'm stupefied, pants around ankles. A quivering hairless wiener three feet from a mother's face. A needle clenched between her lips. She's been quilting. A thread is dangling from the needle. She says, "Lord," and spins away.

After a moment, she sounds very composed behind the door. "Get dressed, honey. It's time for your scout meeting." Ten minutes later, driving me to Scoutmaster Gary's house, she licks her palm and smooths down my hair.

✳

Gary invited my cousin and me over to discuss the requirements for a merit badge in knot tying. We watch the video 10, starring Dudley Moore, instead.

Early in the film, Bo Derek's nipples can be seen through her swimsuit. Later she is completely nude in order to give Dudley Moore's character intercourse. It's wonderful to see. My cousin and I had not yet seen people enjoying intercourse.

When Gary's wife brings in a tray of ice cream, Gary quickly shuts the video off. Then the wife tiptoes back upstairs, and Gary pulls a photograph from an empty album sleeve. "Take a look." The photograph features a woman dancing naked in what looks like a motel room. She is covered with foamy white soap, some of which she is putting in her mouth.

My cousin asks why the woman wants soap in her mouth.

"When you're really turned on," Gary explains, "you'll eat anything."

✳

My sister's first project as Vice President is to orchestrate a castration. My colt has taken an alleged liking to her horse. "He tried to rape her!" While my sister supplies me with instructions, I consider the timing. My very first orgasm had arrived just moments earlier, while my sister and I read a Nancy Drew mystery.

I was wearing Dolphin brand running shorts. They are silky smooth, essentially the same material as panties. They did very little to hide an erection that felt like it'd been in place for several days. When I crossed my legs, the shorts grazed the tip of wood just right, and I had what I thought was an epileptic seizure, accompanied by mighty bursts of thick fantastic urine. I couldn't determine whether my sister understood what was happening, because I didn't understand what was happening.

She scooted away. "What are you doing, spaz?"

I groaned "Nothing" and tried not to flop around, then hurried to the bathroom. So this is what all that *finding yourself* talk is about. By rubbing against material, you get to unload spicy product all over yourself. I cleaned up and immediately gave it another shot, dragging a towel back and forth across the control tower. Blast off! But one problem. The towel was terry cloth, so this time the murky white magic was laced with blood.

My sister informed me of the attempted rape of her horse as I exited the bathroom, so I figure *she* feels violated, having witnessed the magnificent man-violence in my girl-shorts. She wants me castrated, but my horse is the next best thing.

I will go to Dad, she explains, with my decision to remove Saber's nuts. He is getting older anyway, and will start acting wild like all stallions do. Dad will front half the money for the operation because I will promise to work it off. My sister will secure the remaining funds from Mother, who won't require reimbursement. If necessary, my sister will twist her arm. But most likely, her payment will be donated gladly, simply to discourage erotic violation of family pets by other family pets.

A telephone rigged to the horn of the veterinarian's truck goes off as he prepares the hypodermic. Saber bolts across the field. I go and get him. I bring him back so the vet can open his ball sack with elbowed scissors, then use a type of pruning shear to sever the first cord. It crunches like an Achilles tendon.

He lifts out a huge clean testicle and lobs it to the edge of the lawn. The second one is not fully distended. He has to reach into Saber's body cavity. He chops and yanks out what looks like a bloody distributor cap, then tosses it beside its brother.

"Easy enough, right?" He smiles at me and sprinkles white powder into the emptied scrotum, which he doesn't sew shut.

*

Dad is counting out one-dollar bills on the front porch.

The vet is rubbing Buffy's stomach.

I whisper, "She has cancer."

"What?"

"She has cancer in her uterus. Another vet said that, but my dad doesn't want to do anything. He doesn't want to pay for it. She's been falling down like she's having heart attacks."

The vet glances at Dad mouthing numbers, then prods Buffy's abdomen. "You'll have to bring her in. I won't charge for the examination, but an operation is a different story."

"How much is an operation?"

"How much you got?"

I shrug.

"I'm just kidding. We'll deal with that when we figure out what's wrong. Here's my card. If you need a ride . . ."

Dad walks up.

The vet hands me the card. "Like I said, if your colt isn't standing in half an hour, it's the second number there."

Dad counts the money onto the hood of the truck, then says, "He's twenty dollars short."

"Who is?"

Dad gestures to me.

The vet asks, "Is this your money?"

"I'm borrowing it."

He nods for a moment. "OK."

✳

I race over because chickens are pecking at the testicles on the lawn. The rooster stands his ground a moment, so I try to kick his goddamn head off, but miss. I want to carry the testicles to Saber, moaning in his sleep, but can't bring myself to touch them. Silvery pink and veiny. So I just lie beside Saber and stand guard.

The chickens poke around in the field and keep glancing over, but I've lost sight of the delusional rooster. He's black with white spots, and has no idea that he's a chicken. He attacks everything. He charges our car. He fights with Buffy. When Mother forgets to carry a broom, he flaps up and tries to gouge her.

Saber is starting to move when I hear the patter of little feet. The rooster is attacking from my blind spot, launching with claws spread forward in hopes of landing on my face. I punch him out of the air, then chase him around the yard until I can't breathe.

The rooster struts next to the shed.

I pick up a small rock and muster all the hate in the world.

Eyes, I learn, do not actually get *put out*. They sort of pop and pour blood. The rooster staggers in a circle, leaning in as if the lack of an eye is very heavy, then trots out of sight.

Saber is standing. He snorts and shakes his head, then wobbles toward the barn. He won't stop to let me hug his neck. I have to apologize on the move. This is the second time I hear the voices. The first time, I dismissed it as a fluke, but here they are again—a murmuring crowd, with endless information if only I could decipher mumble. They're encouraging me to step aside. Not surrender, especially. It doesn't feel like surrender, though it might be. I strain to make out a single word, but it's a haze of dead grandparents translated into impulse. They are pretending to advise me because they know what's going to happen, but end up just judging me and complaining. It's a spiteful group with terrible advice, but, transposed as feeling, it's impossible to dispute. That's the difficulty with emotion. You can't disagree. So I try to drown it out by humming.

Saber leans against the barn wall, head down, and moans for two days. While digging a shallow grave for his balls, it occurs to me that my sister hadn't actually threatened me this time. There was no threat because it's no longer necessary. My training is complete. She can ask me to do great bodily harm to something I love, and I cannot locate the word *no*. Not because of specific fear any more, but because my range of possibility has been meticulously chopped away. I would make a wonderful Nazi.

Before the rooster's eye even heals, he learns to attack sideways like a crab, leading with his good eye. Dad finally puts him in a burlap sack and drops him into the river.

Chapter 21

After coaching each Mormon boys basketball game, Scout-master Gary coaches the postgame showers. He hands out shampoo and analyzes why we lost so miserably. He stands by while we soap up and plans strategy while we dry off.

This time he sits next to my cousin and me to let us in on something. It's a serious matter, so we have to keep quiet about it. One of the scouts, the best player on the team, confided in him about an incident. The boy cannot go to his father, who is an Elder in the church, because his father might blame him for what happened.

In the middle of the night, Gary says, while the boy slept, an intruder came into his room. The intruder cupped his hand over the boy's mouth and did things to him. He did everything he wanted to. And the boy could do nothing because he was afraid.

Gary tells us not to worry. He will do his best to make sure the same thing doesn't happen to us. "I'm keeping my eye on you two."

He stands and makes an announcement. He anoints my cousin and me *Scouts of the Month* and awards us a special outing. We will visit Gary's cabin in the mountains and sleep overnight. Just the three of us. Then he twists a damp towel in a whip and tries to thwack our buttocks.

*

It's a two-hour drive through severe wind, which keeps nudging Gary's truck into the wrong lane. The cabin is surrounded by pine trees the height and width of telephone poles, but not as sturdy. They bow more than I thought trees could bow. Gary unlocks the cabin door and says that in Vietnam the wind had been much worse. This is nothing. In Vietnam, the wind tipped over hovering helicopters and killed everyone waiting to climb in.

Then he takes out a special deck of cards to ease our minds about the storm. He will show us how to play poker. The backs of his cards feature photos of people having all types of sex. He deals the cards and says that his good buddy had been smashed by a tree in Vietnam. He held the man's hand while he died. It was something he will never forget. The promises he made. The look on the man's face.

Then a tree cracks in the distance and whooshes to the

ground. Gary looks nervous. He's never heard trees fall here before. If a tree lands on the cabin and smashes him, he instructs us to not wait around and hold his hand while he dies. We should jump in the truck and get the hell out of here. Neither of us mention that we can't drive yet. We are busy with the marvelous information stored on the cards.

Hairy things being put into other hairy things. Some hair in the process of being shaved off. Women's faces between the legs of other women. We consider Gary a good friend for showing us things that no one else will.

Another tree falls. Gary glances out the window, then suggests we play strip poker.

We shake our heads no.

"Then maybe I should take the cards away."

My cousin leans in and whispers, "Let's just play until we get down to underwear. Then we'll quit."

But we don't need to quit. I turn out to be an expert poker player. Gary loses almost every hand. He's soon naked from the waist down, having removed his underwear before his socks and shirt. His penis is hard and small, peeking out below his stomach fat. I have lost only my shoes. Few of the cards feature only two people. I'm amazed by all the different things they can do. The ladies look relaxed and happy about all the variations, while the men seem to strain with concentration.

My cousin is losing. He gets down to his underwear, then surprises me by removing them.

Gary has a remark waiting. "Nice and long for a boy your age."

This embarrasses my cousin, but he's glad to hear it. We both worry that we still have baby penises.

Now it's time, Gary says, to "play for sucks."

My cousin looks at me and laughs, then waits for my answer, which is this:

"Nah."

Gary nods a moment. "Don't worry, it'll be fun."

Another tree snaps during the next hand, and Gary stares at the ceiling as if waiting to be smashed. The tree lands directly next to the cabin and makes some extra noise. Gary stands and looks out the window, fat-assed, holding his cards. The tree, on its way down, struck another tree, which dropped a thick branch onto the hood of the truck.

"OK," Gary says. "Time to go."

My parents want to know why I'm home early, and why I'm not wearing shoes.

I say, "We had to leave in a hurry because there were trees falling all over the place. That's all."

Chapter 22

Mother applies dark lipstick. "Put on your church clothes, kids. We've only got half an hour and the roads are pure ice." My sister and brother go to their rooms like it makes perfect sense. Mother sits to spend the interval quilting. I stand in the center of the room and listen for Dad. I've obviously missed something crucial. "Where's Dad?"

"Don't worry, honey. I took care of it. Things are back to normal."

I find Buffy beside the chicken coop. She wags her tail and scoots forward. Dad is patching a hole in the chicken wire.

"Mom says we're going to church...."

Dad bangs the coop to scare back the curious chickens. "Yeah?"

Buffy sits up and raises a paw to shake. I ask, "Is something wrong?"

Dad fits wire over the hole and secures it on each side, then snips the excess. "Nope."

✴

The usher's hands are as big as his head. He raises fingers for each arriving family to signal how many seats are left in a particular row. An old woman plays an upbeat death march on the chapel organ. Mother works the room like a class reunion, hugging and laughing. When the organ stops, she joins us in the last row.

The red-haired Bishop steps to the podium. "I want to extend a warm welcome to the Jamison family. It's good to see them again."

Mom mouths *Thank you* to the Bishop, then to the few heads that turn with supportive nods.

The Bishop announces that Scoutmaster Gary "will no longer be involved in church functions." When the new Scoutmaster is introduced, he receives no applause. Mormons don't believe in clapping.

Gary has been arrested. I whisper to Mother, "How could he be involved? He's in jail."

"When he gets out, the Bishop will excommunicate him."

Then the Bishop proclaims it a very special Sunday. God has apparently changed his mind about all the African American business. He sent Word down to the Mormon president,

Spencer W. Kimball, who is spreading the exciting news among Church ranks. "Blacks" will now be considered worthy of holding the priesthood.

Gary was indicted on thirteen felony counts ranging from child endangerment to sodomy to kidnapping. My cousin and I were questioned together, but when my cousin started acting peculiar, the detective split us up.

During my account of the cabin trip, it finally occurred to me that perhaps Gary is not my best friend. According to the detective, my experience was the least severe of any of the boys interviewed so far. Some of them had caught real hell.

Mother heard a rumor that Gary plans to plead guilty in exchange for several years in prison. His wife plans to stand by him. They have two daughters, and she refuses to give up on the marriage, mainly because she is pregnant again.

Then Mother whispers something that I hope none of the other boys will hear. "I knew there was something sick about that man."

She means this:

I am a good mother. I have radar.

But if the boys actually hurt by Gary hear this from their parents, they might misunderstand. They might interpret it the way I do:

I figured something was wrong, and did nothing.

✦

When Mother stands, the usher hurries over with a microphone, his fingers as thick as pickles. It's the first Sunday of the
month, when the congregation takes turns "bearing testimony." After a scripted introduction—"I would like to bear my
testimony that I know this church is true, that Joseph Smith
is the true prophet"—members go on to describe their gratitude for all the blessings of a strong church and family. Parents
pass the microphone to children, and everyone laughs politely
when younger ones mispronounce words or need to be fed a
line. I slump down as Mother's voice fills the chapel.

"Thank you, Bishop, for your kind words. It's good to be
back." She takes a moment to collect her thoughts. "I would
like to bear my testimony that I know this church is true, that
Joseph Smith is the true prophet, that Christ is my savior, and
that my loving children are the light of my life." She beams
down at us, then clenches her lips to avoid crying. "We've had
some difficulties at home recently, but these kids never got discouraged. They held their heads high. When I look at them, I
am filled with such pride and wonder. I'm sorry . . ."

She dabs tears, then presses a fist against her mouth.

A woman next to us holds up tissue.

"Thank you," Mother wipes her cheeks. "These wonderful kids give me such strength and purpose. I don't know what I would do without them. I love them more than I can say. . . ." She can't stop crying, and tries, mid-sob, to hand the microphone to me.

I just stare at my new shoes, the money for which was marked in my debit section of Dad's poetry book. I had asked Dad for shoes for my birthday, but made the mistake of saying I *needed* them for school. He had asked what I *wanted*.

I said, "What's the difference?"

This frustrated him. I should know by now. To clarify the difference, he gave me ski boots four sizes too small from a garage sale. He hand-painted the package with skiers launching from ramps, then left it in the sun. For whatever reason, the sunshine attracted a plague of earwigs. The motion of yanking the box flaps apart sprung the majority of the earwigs into my face. Dad couldn't have been happier. It didn't seem to bother him that I never even tried the boots on. He felt he'd made his point, which he elaborated later in the day—something about not promoting simplemindedness by giving people what they *think* they need.

The real point was that he only cares about two things: the entertainment value of an exchange, and trying to alter someone's perception with disagreeable surprises. He wants to give the impression that he's looking out for us by constantly mixing things up. Keeping us on our toes. But really, he's simply addicted to doing precisely what he wants every stinking minute of the day. So the trick will be to never tell him exactly what I want. Or tell him the opposite of what I want. At least then there's an outside chance I'll get it.

"Please," Mother hisses, mascara blotching under her eyes. So I take the microphone, but I bear no testimony. I stand and give it back to Pickle Fingers, who offers me a disapproving smile.

Sitting down, practically falling, Mom weeps into her hands.

Someone else starts to speak.

My sister elbows me and makes this assessment:

"Shit for brains."

✳

Mother hums the final hymn all the way home.

Dad is gone, along with Buffy.

My sister and brother start watching cartoons.

Mother returns to her quilt.

I ask, "Where did he take Buffy?"

My brother turns and waits for Mother's answer. It doesn't come, so my brother answers, "For the operation . . ."

Dad opens the front door after dark. "I need to talk to you kids."

My sister and brother follow him into the kitchen.

I look out the window, then stare at Mother. She didn't even glance up when Dad came in. She can't stop quilting. "Where's Buffy?" I ask. "What did he do?"

She snips a piece of thread. "Go talk to him, honey."

I go outside and check under the house. "Buffy!" But if she had the operation, she wouldn't be moving around. I go back inside, where my brother is now crying on Mother's lap. My sister is kicking a wall in her room.

Dad is tight-lipped and pale in the kitchen. His fists are on the table. He says that a second estimate had come in. The surgery would've cost two hundred and forty dollars. So he drove Buffy to a truck stop.

"What?"

He opened a ten-pound bag of dog food and left it with her.

"Where?"

"Someone will find her and take her home."

"Where?"

"Listen to me!"

I don't. I run to the living room and grab my new shoes, then scream at Mother on my way back. "You knew!"

She is humming that final hymn into my brother's hair.

Dad's face is in his hands.

"OK." I pull on a shoe. "Where is she?"

"Just listen a second."

"Tell me where, you fucking idiot!"

"Goddamn it, listen!" He snatches my other shoe and heaves it sideways, through the kitchen window. The shattering sound stuns us both. One jagged piece of glass is left.

Dad opens his mouth, but I'm running again. Past Mother rocking my brother. Past my sister smashing something in her room, and out the front door. Gravel jabs my one bare foot.

Dad storms through the door as I mount my bike, so I pedal like a madman. "Where is she?!"

"It's ten miles!" He chases me, but I pick up serious speed by picturing the good-bye:

Buffy confused and freezing next to a public toilet. Dad simply driving away, waving. Buffy chasing the truck. Dad yelling out the window, "No, girl! Sit! Stay!"

But the sound of his voice, I know for certain, only made her run harder.

Chapter 23

Mother cries quietly through our first breakfast in the new house that we all helped build. Dad already sold it, but is negotiating a delayed transfer of property, which will allow us a few months of counterfeit American-dream bliss.

Mother is at the stove when I ask what's wrong.

She says, "He had to tell me last night. He couldn't even let me sleep one night in my own house."

＊

The veterinarian meets me at a gas station, expecting Buffy. My request irritates him, but when we find the bag of dog food at a truck stop in Durkee, he seems spooked. He just stares at the bag next to a drinking fountain while I wander around yelling for Buffy.

I ask people if they've seen her, but they've stopped only long enough to shit and buy soda from a machine.

I tell the vet about a television program featuring dogs that find their way home no matter what. Hundreds of miles.

He says, "Somebody probably took her."

"She's not a friendly dog."

"You'd be surprised. I'm sure she was scared, and with the highway right here, I doubt she made a run for it. I'll bet somebody took her home. I'll check the pound tomorrow. And I'll post something at my office. She'll turn up. They probably knew she was abandoned because of the bag of dog food."

"Then why didn't they take the bag?"

"Yeah. I don't know."

✹

Mother decides to take a full-time job to help with the mortgage. She thinks this might change Dad's mind by easing the financial pressure.

Dad misunderstands and dissolves Economy Builders, thinking Mother's job is a replacement for his. He fires himself and takes a decoy job at the hospital as a part-time janitor, claiming that it's the only work he can find. Really, it's the only work that offers him unlimited access to cafeteria leftovers. In exchange for a couple hours of sweeping each day, Dad receives a key to the padlock on the hospital dumpster.

Our meals are soon fifty percent garbage again. Camouflage is especially important since hospital food is rarely pack-aged. All of Mother's groceries are stripped down and sealed in zip-lock bags. Wrapperless and frozen brick-solid, garbage and food look identical.

Mother questions some of the choices—"Who freezes chocolate bars?"—but doesn't get suspicious until Dad serves up banana enchiladas. He figured the frozen brown stuff was meat. Then, while enjoying one of those delicious chocolate bars, Mother notices that it's laced with frozen worms the length and thickness of eyelashes. She spends the remainder of the weekend in her bedroom.

✦

Dad pretends to be doing something janitorial—jumping up and down to make more room in the dumpster—while a doc-tor tosses in a paper coffee cup. They talk a minute, and the doctor says, "Oh, you're Dirk's father. You know what, I think your son is in love with my daughter."

I've been hanging around his house. His daughter's name is Beth. She is beautiful and kind, and I spend a ridiculous amount of time concocting good reasons to stand next to her. She plays bass in band, which places her within three feet of me for a full hour. But the acknowledgment by the doctor somehow screws it up. I keep picturing the two fathers talking together after a day's work. One just finished with delicate brain surgery. The other just discovered four quarts of perfectly good coleslaw. I have no business loving his daughter.

So I avoid Beth and pursue a girl who helped me get my first non-A by caressing my faithful erections during typing class. We sat in the last row, with her sweater draped over my lap. I eventually earned a C for typing orgasmic gibberish. She received a D for typing one-handed.

※

My report card arrived the same day I got arrested for shoplifting acne cream. Dad rewards all straight-A report cards with Peanut Buster Parfaits from Dairy Queen. Skipping a grade in math had gotten me a sleeping bag designed for ten degrees below zero. But on this day, Dad offered only one sentence regarding my arrest. It might've been curiosity—an invitation to elaborate—but I took it as criticism.

"Your mother told me you cried."

The skin problems of other kids my age amount to extra freckles. Faint pink dots on their cheeks. But my face has quickly adopted the look of third-degree infectious disease. Pimples are born deep in cartilage, hard as marbles, and swell up half my face. I tell girls that I ran into a door to explain the core zit bulging my nose like a neon ad for ugly.

So I pocketed some Apri Facial Scrub. But my down parka, since it was eighty degrees outside, gave me away.

Mother picked me up when the cop finished his interrogation. It was my first theft, and she wasn't angry. She only felt guilty, knowing I would never break the law if I had enough money to obey it.

She offered me an allowance. She would come up with the money somehow. She promised me three dollars a week, and I could purchase as much acne scrub as I liked. This is when the crying started. The cop had scared me, so I was already on the verge. But it was the sincerity in Mom's voice that really got me going. It sounded like she wanted me to have what I needed.

*

The vet calls to say that he might've found Buffy. He just removed a cancerous uterus from a German shepherd that a family brought in. She's still in his office, so I can go down and identify her.

I ask, "They paid for the operation?"

"Yeah."

The voice is mine, but I'm not choosing the words. "Let her stay with them."

"What? Don't you want to find out if it's her?"

"Are they nice?"

"What?"

"Are the people nice?"

"Yeah, they seem nice. They have a little girl."

"OK."

✳

Mother is depressed. She realizes this when a car almost runs her down. I find her sitting in the living room with all the drapes closed. She's doing nothing. No quilting. No embroidery. She says, "How was school?"

"What happened?"

"You're so intuitive, honey. You always know when something is wrong."

"Well, the drapes are all . . ."

"Don't tell anybody, but this car came screeching around a corner today. I had to dive out of the way. But when I was picking myself up, I thought, 'You stupid idiot, why did you do that?'"

"Who, the driver?"

"No, me. Why did I get out of the way?" She stares a moment. "I missed my period last month, so I thought I was pregnant. And when I told your father, he said he wanted to get an abortion. I guess I should've expected that. It doesn't matter now because I started my period yesterday. Probably all the stress lately just messed up my cycle. But now I can't stop thinking about his reaction. I guess it kind of broke my heart. I understand why people get abortions when they're young, but how can you do that once you've had kids. You know what I mean? Think about your little brother. What if we didn't have him? That's what I told your father. What if we had aborted your little brother? But it still didn't change his mind. I don't know. I guess this isn't something you need to hear about. So how was school?"

Chapter 24

To commemorate the divorce, we move into a blue shitbox near the center of town. Filing the divorce papers upset Mother enough that she didn't bother with the details. Dad was unable to sell our new house outright. The best he could do was swap it for this shitbox, plus $20,000 cash, which finds its way into Dad's pocket. He gives Mother the shitbox because it's been on the market without a nibble for two years. He is going back to California.

*

When Dad's first marriage ended in the sixties, it was arranged that he pay child support. Rather than find another place to live, Dad slept in the escrow office where he worked. In the morning, he boiled eggs in the coffeemaker. "The secretaries got really pissed off about that."

Then Jean, his ex-wife, moved to Bass Lake, California, for

a teaching job, so Dad stopped sending the child support because she was making "teacher money now."

Six months later, one of his sons got in trouble for running a stolen tractor through someone's yard. He was taken to
juvenile hall, so Dad drove up to help. "But when I got there,
they said 'Ah ha! We got you now!' And they put *me* in jail."

Dad was charged with desertion. Due to blinding anger,
he refused to let Jean bail him out. He felt he'd been tricked.
The truth was, Jean had become terminally ill without telling anyone. She was collecting welfare, which required her to
file papers against her deadbeat ex-husband. She felt bad, and
brought Dad a guitar so he would have something to do in jail.
He played songs through the weekend.

"But I only knew a few songs, so the other guys in there
got a little irritated and told me to shut the hell up. Then
Monday morning I saw the judge. He said, 'You're bad and
you gotta pay this.' I told him I couldn't. He said, 'Well, you're
gonna have to!' But then he let me go without paying a dime.
It's weird. I guess they figure if they scare you, you'll just pay.
But I got out of there scot-free. In fact, they owed me money because you get a certain amount per day for being in the
slammer. So they said, 'We'll owe it to you.' And I said, 'Yeah,
I'll owe it to you too!'"

✴

The paperwork for his current divorce says this:

> Marital status is terminated and the parties are restored
> to the status of unmarried persons. This proceeding
> was heard as uncontested. It is further ordered that the
> Respondent shall pay to the Petitioner a sum as child
> support, payable on the 15th of each month, continu-
> ing until said children reach maturity, or are eman-
> cipated, or die. The total amount for child support is
> $150.00 monthly.

Dad says this: "Yeah, right."

✴

The night before Dad leaves, I dream of standing in the bed of
his pickup. The rest of the family is in the cab. It's dark and I'm
freezing. There are low street lamps that require me to duck
down every fifty yards. When I spot Buffy, I bang the cab roof,
but the truck doesn't slow down. I bang several dents until
losing sight of her, then notice the next street lamp coming.

But this time when I duck, I really duck, and crack my face against something. My new bedroom is the basement with no door separating it from the garage. I sleep on a foam pad on the floor. In the center of the room is a wooden post. This is what cracks my face.

Blood is making its way into my pajama pants as I tiptoe past Dad sleeping on the couch, then past Mother because the only bathroom is in the master bedroom.

The amount of blood makes the gash look fake. It's horizontal, right between the eyes. I spread it open and see white, which doesn't compute, so I lean in for a better look. It's bone. I'm looking at my skull.

I black out for a moment against the wall, but succeed in waking neither parent. I use three butterfly bandages left over from Mammoth, then wrap my head in gauze and go back to bed.

❋

Dad laughs about the abundance of gauze in the morning. "I guess you didn't control *that* dream, huh?"

I help him pack the truck. He shows me a brochure entitled *Build Yourself a Modern Sea-Going Polynesian Catamaran*. He has enough cash to buy a boat and start sailing immediately, but he plans to buy wood instead. Bob has proposed his side yard as a building site. The brochure offers construction blueprints for a whopping three hundred dollars, so Dad will draw them himself by referring to a rough sketch in the foldout section of the brochure. The sketch features a young woman at the helm of her new catamaran, charting an intelligent course. She is topless.

✳

My brother and sister sob their way back to the house after hugging Dad. It's the first time I've seen my sister cry. Mother is waiting for them in the doorway. She refuses to say good-bye.

Dad starts the truck and lets it warm up, staring into the distance for a moment. "When I was about seventeen, my mom would get after me to mow the lawn on Saturday. We had a good-sized lawn. But I didn't want to do it because I wanted to go diving. Paul Garrison was my best friend, and we always went diving down at Pales Verdes for abalone. So my dad would get himself involved somehow. He would tell me, 'Well, you can either mow the lawn, or go diving.' He would give me the option. So obviously I went diving. He gave me that freedom. And with him there was never any recrimination. When I came back from diving, there was no blame or guilt from him."

"Who mowed the lawn?"

"Yeah, exactly!" Dad laughs. "That's the point. I got to go this magical place, which is gone now. They started dumping raw sewage in Pales Verdes and killed all the sea life. But it was beautiful back then, and it's still very vivid in my head."

"Who mowed it?"

"My mom did! But she's the one that wanted it mowed in the first place! And I'm sure somebody's still mowing that goddamn lawn."

✦

The truck is warm. Dad hands me a parting gift—a *Certificate of Freedom*, written on the back of thick hospital stationary. He used a brown felt-tip pen to imitate the look of calligraphy:

This proclamation hereby declares that Dirk Jamison, as of this moment, and including all future moments, is free.

He says, "Once I get the boat started, I want you to come down and help. That sounds fun, right?"

"Good luck, Dad."

"What do you mean?

"Nothing. Just good luck."

"Hey, remember, I wanna be like you when I grow up."

"OK. Bye."

Chapter 25

My first postcard from Dad shows a pristine beach on the edge of a Mexican jungle. He tucked the card into an envelope so Mother couldn't read it.

Dirk,

My best friend from childhood is dead. An answer to my "Hi, Paul, you old fart" note came from his widow—as I remember, the ugliest woman on Earth (except for your mother the day she nearly drowned and sobbed, "You almost lost me!" Her hair was covered with sand and she looked like a water buffalo). Anyway, a second bypass operation caught Paul Garrison with his shorts down and he went to Jesus about 6 months ago. I'm spearing fish with a Hawaiian sling and playing my guitar at night. I'm camping in an abandoned concrete lighthouse, so my guitar echoes like a son of a bitch.

Love, Dad

P.S. Be a winner, son. Always give between 65 and 70 percent.

Epilogue

I decide to take spring break in Glen Avon, California, where the boat is docked in Bob's gravel driveway, sixty miles from open ocean. I haven't seen Dad for over a year. He meets me at the train station, and we walk against a brutal wind through the rattiest residential neighborhood in America. Almost every yard is protected by at least two raving pit bulls, which bounce against chicken wire fences to prove how much they want to kill us. Dad claims the dogs are inexpensive alarm systems for crystal-meth labs disguised as trailer homes.

I expect something spectacular, but the boat is just a gigantic plywood canoe. And it's not Dad's. Bob started it, but made some catastrophic design mistake. Dad is here to dismantle it and reuse the lumber to start his own boat in the vacant lot next door.

I ask, "Why's the wind so bad out here?"

"The Santa Anas! It's supposed get even worse tonight, and it's gonna rain. My damn tarps are all over the place. Come on, you can sleep in the boat. It's a real treat. I'll sleep in my van." He leads me to a homemade wooden ladder. Ropes and tarps are flapping against the hull. A green kayak has blown down from its rack, and a dog is howling nonstop next door.

Dad says, "That damn mutt over there. He's tied in the middle of the field. There's nothing around except a tree, so the BBs don't make a sound."

Dad bought a BB gun at a flea market. His aim is worthless, but the BB usually pings against something and startles the dogs. When nobody is looking, he shoots during the day, even if there's no barking. This way the dogs clearly see a gun pointed at them, which they instinctively hate. Dad wants them to associate the pop of the gun with the sight of it, so during some barking craze at three in the morning, he can just fire into darkness and the dogs will understand.

"I tried shooting that mutt during the day, but he's too dumb! I even nailed him a couple times, but he's so furry he can't feel anything. I finally figured it out, though. He barks when he's hungry. The people there don't feed him. So you know that big slingshot I have?"

"Yeah." We used to launch water balloons with it. You step on a tab sewn into the pouch and pull the rubber straps up. The balloons go so high that nobody can tell where they're coming from.

"I've been shooting hamburgers to him."

"What?"

"That shuts him up."

"You slingshot hamburgers?"

"Yeah, from the dumpsters. I leave them in the wrapper, otherwise they fly apart."

"The dog unwraps?"

"Isn't that great? I can't see a thing at night, so I just aim for the tree. If I hit that, the burger usually falls where he can get at it."

"Don't the owners find the wrappers?"

"They don't pay attention! They wouldn't notice if the dog died! The funny thing is, when I first shot something over, I was trying to kill him. I feel sort of bad now, but I mixed rat poison into some raw hamburger. When he stopped barking, I thought he was dead. But in the morning, there he was. Sicker than a dog! And I finally realized he's just hungry."

"Jesus, Dad."

He laughs until he starts coughing. "Yeah, I shot him, then poisoned him, and now I'm feeding him! Whatever works, right?"

I climb to the deck of the boat.

"Hey, take this in case the dogs keep you awake." Dad comes halfway up the ladder to hand me the BB gun. "You gotta pump it about ten times."

I open the hatch. The wind tries to shut it.

"Feel free to shoot Bob's dogs too. They love it! I nailed one of them the other day, but it was a different kind of BB. It's got this pointed end on it, so I had to dig it out of her haunch with tweezers."

"Did she love it?"

"You betcha! Hey, thanks for coming. I found this old chain saw. If we can get it working, we can start tearing this beast down. I'll see you in the morning. There's plenty of food in there if you get hungry tonight."

My nose goes numb after a sneezing fit from all the dust, so it takes a few minutes to fully appreciate the stifling decay. It's like being inside a wooden spine full of sweet rot. Crates of nearly black bananas. A pile of mangoes bleeding juice as thick as sap. Pineapples bending forward like old men because their centers have liquefied. A bag of potatoes growing desperate vines through the burlap. All the apples have a black eye, and every orange wears a skullcap of mold.

Something is slapping against the hull. I sit and listen to the wind build momentum, inadvertently asking what has lately become my proverbial question:

What the hell are you doing?

Mother was pissed when I left. She doesn't want me making the same mistakes Dad has. She worries I'll get brainwashed because Dad is so good at convincing people that he's "a guru or something."

"An enlightened person does not live the kind of life your father has. He wants to get all the free cheese and butter he can, and he thinks that means he's fooling the system. That's not an enlightened person."

"I know, Mom."

"That's a person who's afraid to compete. He's afraid to go out and prove the intelligence he has. He has a good IQ, but he's afraid to do anything with it. An enlightened person has joy and feeling to give back. Your father has nothing to give back. You probably think he gives you love, but only in ways that don't cost him anything."

"I know."

"Then why do you take such an interest in him when he's been such a selfish jerk? What did he ever do? It was always me paying the bills and keeping the heat going. I crawled under the house and unfroze the pipes when he went on those chickenshit vacations to Baja! I worked really hard for Christmas and all your clothes for school. What did your father do? He did whatever the hell he wanted, that's what! And now you're going down to help him with the stupid boat! I'm working two jobs, and you're spending your money to go help him. I don't understand it, Dirk! What did he do to deserve all this?"

"I don't know, Mom."

The slapping sound has doubled, and dogs have commenced a barking frenzy, which suddenly floods me with a white-hot, inexplicable rage. I would love to kill something right now, so I rise up out of the hatch, pumping the BB gun like a maniac, and firing at nothing.

"Whoa, son of a bitch! Watch where you're shooting!" Dad is standing at one end of the hull, wrestling with the corner of a tarp that has blown loose. The barking is courtesy of Bob's dogs. They're upset about the tarp flapping above the boat like a giant blue ghost. Dad yells, "Help me reel this sucker in!"

I grab another corner, which only makes the tarp swell up and catch the wind full force. "Hey!" Dad laughs. "I'll bet this is what sailing is like!"

We have to let go, or we'll get jerked overboard.

Dad and me, 1967

Dad and me, 1994